BEST OF

LONELY PLANET
TRAVEL WRITING

EDITED BY TONY WHEELER

LONELY PLANET PUBLICATIONS
MELBOURNE • OAKLAND • LONDON

Best of Lonely Planet Travel Writing
Published by Lonely Planet Publications

Head Office:
90 Maribyrnong Street, Footscray, Vic 3011, Australia
Locked Bag 1, Footscray, Vic 3011, Australia

Branches:
150 Linden Street, Oakland CA 94607, USA
2nd Floor, 186 City Road, London ECV1 2NT, UK

Published 2009
Printed by China Translation and Printing Services Ltd
Printed in China

National Library of Australia Cataloguing-in-Publication entry

Best of Lonely Planet Travel Writing/editor Tony Wheeler

ISBN 978 1 74179 511 0 (pbk)

1. Travelers' writings 2. Voyages and travels – anecdotes

910.4

CONTENTS

Contents

INTRODUCTION

Your own experience and someone else's – travel needs both. We want to go there ourselves, taste the food, ride the buses, crash in the hotel rooms, meet the people. We shove our guidebook into our daypack and head off to collide with those events. Then we want the other perspective – how some other traveller reacted to that appalling meal, that nightmare bus ride, that horror-story of a hotel. And did they also have that fleeting midnight encounter? Why didn't she turn up at the bar the next evening? Will she be there at the next town down the line?

I love guidebooks. I've been involved in writing plenty of them and even more have taken up residence in my daypack. There's almost always one by my bedside – research material for the next trip or a taster for somewhere further down the line. But the literature of travel, those books which document somebody else's travels, experiences, fears, hopes and inspirations are equally important for me. They're part introduction to places I'm planning to go, part inspiration for trips I may one day make, and part reminders of past trips – a different interpretation of a shared experience.

Some places simply seem to inspire great travel writing. It's no surprise that writers zero in on Italy or Australia. They're great places to travel, they attract many visitors and they provide abundant material to work with. Both feature in this collection. On the other hand, my travel bookshelves feature a surprising number of books on Afghanistan and that African nation currently known as the Democratic Republic of Congo (the name a hint that it's one of those places where democracy has a hard time). Both countries seem to bring out the best in travel writers and although I've made a couple of extraordinarily interesting visits to Afghanistan, I've still not set foot in the Congo. At the moment those African titles are on my shelves purely as inspiration for trips yet to come.

There are a number of tales in this collection from countries that are not exactly tourist favourites. Places more likely to feature in government travel advisories warning you off from even thinking of going there, than in travel brochures enticing you to sign up for the next departure. In fact, my experience has been that these countries are rarely as dangerous as they're made out to be. As well as Nicholas Crane's Afghan odyssey in 'Finding Shelter', Syria, Ethiopia, Central African Republic and Iraq all pop up in this book and their entry stamps have all appeared in my passport.

Travel is as much about mood and event as it is place. In our travel anthologies over the years, the recurring themes of travel have been just as important as the places our talented writers have used as their backdrops. I have a special fondness for travel out on the edge, to unlikely places and nervous destinations. My own book *Bad Lands*, which started with a trip along the former US president's much-loved – by edge-loving travellers at least – 'Axis of Evil', heads in that direction and so do some of the accounts we gathered together in *Tales from Nowhere*. I particularly liked Jason Elliot's 'A Visit to Kanasankatan', which turned out to be an edgy sort of place in a most unexpected location. On the other hand, Laura Resau's 'Secrets of the Maya' confirmed my theory that places are never as edgy as they seem at first glance. No matter where you are, Karl Taro Greenfeld's 'On the Trail' confirmed that most basic advice for modern life: back everything up.

Spend enough time on the road and it's inevitable that at some point things won't work out. Fortunately, somebody often pops up to sort out your problems, and that's what happens in the tales we collected in *The Kindness of Strangers*. I've had plenty of experience with this phenomenon. Looking back on my first 24 hours in Australia – after landing on a beach in Western Australia after a yacht trip down from Bali – it seemed to have been a procession of strangers performing acts of kindness. It's no wonder I've been trying to repay that karma ever since because, as James D Houston points out so succinctly in 'Everything Come Round'…it does. Simon Winchester's 'Ascension in the Moonlight' is simply wonderful, a little glimpse at those once-in-a-lifetime moments that travel sometimes nonchalantly tosses at our feet.

The travellers' tales we collected for *By the Seat of My Pants* often seemed to end with that moment where you put the palm of your hand to your head and emit a long, drawn out 'duh!'. I'm sure that was the noise Danny Wallace produced after his encounter with a friendly (if Uzi-toting) Czech con-man in 'The Sights of Prague'. Once he'd got his underpants back on, Joshua Clark no doubt made the same comment about his outback Australia car crash in 'Wangara's Cross', a tale with a poignant concluding twist.

Our travelling lives all start somewhere, and kicking off as a young, penniless backpacker is a pretty good way to do it, as the two stories from *Rites of Passage* illustrate. Karen Lee Boren's 'The Quest' is a great description of one of those backpacker hellholes that years down the track you can file away as an experience you're glad you've had, because now you never need have it again. Greg Tuleja's 'A Slight Leaning Backward' is a fine reminiscence of a magic spell in Paris, with a sad little after note.

'Getting there is half the fun' is an aphorism that I've certainly found to be true and it's never been more apposite than right now, when we're all wondering if we're flying more than the world can cope with. *Flightless* concentrated on travel at surface level, whether that means taking the boat, the bus, the bicycle or setting out to see how far our boots will carry us. César Soriano's little train ride from Baghdad to Basra certainly fits the pattern. He could scarcely have found a more uncomfortable way of crossing a war zone; he would also have struggled to make a more interesting trip.

Keen travellers often scratch their heads in bemusement that some of the very best travel tales are about staying in one place. If slow travel – seeing the world at a more reasonable pace – is all the go, then settling down and going absolutely nowhere has to be the ultimate expression of the trend. 'City of Djinns' from our collection *A House Somewhere* tells the tale of a most unlikely holiday home, in Old Delhi. India's one of those places that is always fun to write about, and William Dalrymple certainly has fun with this story.

Travel can go wrong – although if we survive to write about it, it can't have gone too far off track. The tales from *Lonely Planet Unpacked* include my own strange little encounter at the end of Tibet's astonishing Mt Kailash trek. Sometimes, what goes wrong is tied up with the romance we always hope to find on the road, and we explored travel romance both fine (if fleeting) and disastrous in *Brief Encounters*, exemplified here in 'Let's Go', Emily Perkins' slightly stoned visit to Prague.

Bringing together the themes we've explored in our travel anthologies over the years gives a sense of the sheer diversity of travel experiences – that 'anything could happen' thrill that keeps me hitting the road time and time again. I hope this collection inspires you in the same way, whether the trip you're dreaming of is on or off the beaten track, and whatever unexpected kindnesses, adventures or romances you find when you get there.

TONY WHEELER

NO FOOD, NO REST, NO...
PICO IYER

Pico Iyer is the author of several books about the modern world, from *Video Night in Kathmandu* and *The Lady and the Monk* to *The Global Soul* and his most recent work, *The Open Road*, an account of 34 years of talks and travels with the fourteenth Dalai Lama. He tries not to travel with his friend Louis, but somehow they have ended up in Cambodia, Haiti, Morocco, Burma, Turkey and far too many other places (not least the Oakland Coliseum) together. On their most recent trip, to Bolivia, they had a car crash at 3500 metres that left one of them gibbering in nonexistent Spanish and the other training furious glances at their errant driver.

I GOT OFF THE PLANE in Addis Ababa and there, as in so many airports so often in the past, was my school friend Louis, extending a shaky hand. 'This place is pure magic,' he assured me. 'We can go around the whole country with Ethiopian Airlines – the best carrier on the continent – for not much more than $100. The plane stops at five major points of interest, and is perfectly suited to people on their first trip here, with limited means.

'The only other option,' he continued – he was always shrewd in getting to places one day before I did, and so installing himself as boss, with the unquestioned upper hand – 'is to rent a car. This isn't very advisable because there are more car crashes than cars in Ethiopia. Also, they don't have much in the way of roads. The car costs $240 a day, and takes at least 10 days to make the circuit.'

'Excellent,' I said.

'It is,' he said. 'The car's coming for us in two days.'

Travelling with Louis was always a bittersweet experience. The bitterness came at the time, the sweetness in happy retrospect. We'd studied together as teenagers, in a dusty classroom in southern England where we'd played out the whole game of cards from Pope's *Rape of the Lock* and been treated to luscious evocations of *Antony and Cleopatra's* Egypt by an ambiguous teacher. 'The *bhaji* she sat upon' – an inspired transcription of Shakespeare's jewelled 'barge she sat upon' monologue, to capture an England now filled with Indian restaurants – was one of Louis' best party tricks.

Nonetheless, the dilapidated hotel in Paris (Louis walking down the corridor in pyjamas, eliciting tea and sympathy from the staff), the rancid place in Marrakesh (across from the nicest hotel in Africa, where we pretended to be staying), the snowstorm in rural Turkey (the kind locals offering us a daily array of kofta, kofta or meatballs) – none of these experiences had prepared me for this. I'd just flown across the Atlantic from New York on Ethiopian Airlines, and was more than ready to sign up for its frequent-flyer program and ensure free trips to the walled city of Harar for life. The beauty of being on holiday is taking to the air.

'The first point of business,' Louis continued, 'is to fix up a visa for Eritrea.' This was arguably worse news. I'd come all this way in order to see Ethiopia, which was just concluding a shaky peace with neighbouring Eritrea, a country it had been fighting for years. One fruit of this peace was that visas were now available for Eritrea; an added advantage, as I saw it, was that there would be even fewer other visitors to bother us in Ethiopia. Louis, however, had met a man who promised to smooth our way into the Eritrea of his dreams.

It was the day after Christmas, and the streets of Addis Ababa slumbered in a pure blue calm. The weather was as perfect as advertised, and eleven days from now the rending celebrations that mark Christmas in Ethiopia would represent the highlight of the ceremonial year. Few other travellers were in evidence, but the locals were surely delighted to meet a distinguished investment banker (my friend) who was celebrating the chance to pay $2400 for a trip that could be made in greater comfort and with more ease for $240.

'He said that we should just go to his house for coffee, and he'd fix up a visa.'

At this point our benefactor appeared: a shifty man, in clothes almost as shabby as my own, whose eyes were red, though not with tears. 'My friend,' he said, extending his hand towards me. 'Please come.'

His home was appointed with a young woman in very short shorts who was brewing coffee in an atavistic fashion. Our host pointed out her gestures with some delight, and talk passed to Eritrea. As the diplomatic chitchat went on, more young women in very short shorts drifted in and out of the room. Louis looked quite delighted to meet so informal a member of the diplomatic corps.

We were served the ceremonial coffee and felt many eyes upon us.

'The visa to Eritrea...' Louis prompted.

'For that, you must go to the embassy,' our host averred.

Women continued to come and go, talking, as Louis shrewdly noted, of something other than Michelangelo.

'Thank you, my friend,' said our host, looking at us out of the side of his eyes and behaving much as I might at home if a credulous millionaire stopped by for tea. His extended hand was looking for something more than the moist feel of my own.

'It's okay,' Louis said, undeterred, as we went back to the Hotel Ghion, an improbably dark place that, by curious chance, reproduced the name of the festive geisha quarter in Kyoto – though the addition of an 'h' made all the difference between heaven and hell.

'Mohammed Aidid is staying in the hotel.'

Strangely, this was true. Aidid, the Somali warlord who had mocked and savaged American soldiers only a few weeks before in Mogadishu, was, by most accounts, the most wanted man in the world right now. Unlike most fugitives from justice, however, he had decided not to hie himself to Paraguay. He was resident in room 211 of the Ghion, perhaps musing on the comfortable benefits of Ethiopian Airlines.

We went along to his room, but on the subject of visas to Eritrea, the beauty of the day or even the merits of the local coffee, he and his press spokesman were silent.

Louis – in his cream suit and with his reddened complexion resembling, as was his habit, James Bond on an off day – looked forward to the drive ahead of us that was guaranteed to make use of all the clenched teeth and stiff upper lip we had been taught in school, even if the driver couldn't get us to Eritrea.

'There are three laws in international business,' he said (as I remember it, perhaps fictitiously). 'The first is, "Always rent a car from an Italian. Especially if he is a she, and is ready to be asked out to dinner." The second is, "Come to a country where driving is an adventure, nothing like the eventless exercise it is at home". The third is, "Don't bother with discounts when you're on holiday".'

The fourth – it wasn't spoken – is, 'Don't trust an investment banker on anything other than finance'.

Two days later, the blue having hardly risen into the sky, a trim, stiff-backed man with greying hair – Nelson Mandela during his prison years, perhaps – appeared at our door. Behind him was a Toyota Land Cruiser. He took time to show us its amenities. It had locks that didn't engage, seatbelts that didn't close. In the back were two cans of kerosene certain to suffocate us if the roads (or their absence) didn't do the job first.

'Can we play this?' Louis asked, extending a prized copy of *Live Dead* to our new friend and guide.

'Of course, sir,' said the driver, and within seconds the tape player had swallowed the cassette and was spitting out strangled sounds.

Hours later, we were on the road. Our driver possessed a military bearing that inspired confidence in his ability to fight, if not to drive. The car bore the scars of previous trips to remind us that driving in Ethiopia is about as safe as eating a pig on the streets of Kabul. Both car and driver handled with the jittery fitfulness of an automatic-trained novice attempting a stick shift.

'Have you been on this road before?' I asked our leader.

'Yes, sir,' he called back, over the protesting noises of the car. 'Once. Twenty-seven years ago.'

'A long time,' I said.

'Yes, sir. I was a boy then. Travelling by bus.'

Very soon the broken huts and dusty lanes of Addis fell away and we were in the emptiness that is the very soul of Ethiopia. Occasional figures proceeded in a distant line across the emptiness towards the mountains. Petitioners dressed in white walked along the road to far-off churches, to celebrate the season. The purity, the dignity of the place moved me to a deeper part of myself.

The people of Ethiopia have a serious look to them – sharp eyes and heavy beards – and it is easy to feel as if one is moving through the landscape of the Apocrypha in the Bible. People wear crosses and ceremonial scarves over their white clothes. Devotion is intense. The rusted tanks and signs of recent fighting along the road were less potent than the tall, thin figures walking, walking, walking, for weeks, or months, on end.

Our driver allowed us to savour these beauties by flinging the rickety car into top gear and accelerating towards the occasional car that appeared before us, preferably around blind turns.

'What the hell are you up to?' cried Louis.

'Sorry, sir,' he said, and then passed another car to put us into the path of an approaching truck.

'Bloody hell!' said Louis, the counter-intuitive benefits of travelling by road forgotten. 'Are you trying to get us killed?'

'Of course not,' I mentioned to him under my breath. 'If he did, payment would not be forthcoming.'

Our driver saw another madman approaching on the mountain road and went into the wrong lane again, accelerating around the curve.

'I don't believe this!' Louis exclaimed, and then an exchange of words followed that were not diplomatic. We stopped for a little while to catch our breath, and our driver confided, 'Your friend, sir, is very strict. More strict than military.'

'He is,' I conceded. We had already come across travellers who had decided to take the Ethiopian Airlines circuit, looking as if they had enjoyed the holiday of their lives.

The days went on, and often we were caked in dust so as to resemble brown snowmen in the back. To keep the windows closed meant certain death from the cans of kerosene. To open them was to admit all the accumulated sand and grit of centuries. Jerry Garcia would have sweetened the trip considerably, but he was now a pinched squeal of swallowed tape in the Land Cruiser's once state-of-the-art sound system.

'Let's just get to the nearest town and bail out,' said Louis, who looked very close to accepting that there was a benefit in paying less and enjoying more. For a dangerous moment I felt that English masochism was going to accept defeat in the wilds of Ethiopia.

Fortunately, our driver protected us from this. 'No lunch,' he began to wail piteously, when informed of the new hurry-up plan.

'No breakfast, no lunch, no rest.'

'No end,' said Louis bitterly, and with that, communications between the two broke down for good. From then on, for day after day on unpaved roads, the Land Cruiser sending us jolting against its uneven roof, the kerosene directing the perfumes of Araby into our nostrils, the new jolts shaking the dust from us, the sand getting inside our eyes and ears, as if we were crossing the Sahara on camel, both my companions chose to speak only through an intermediary.

'Tell him to slow down,' said Louis, as we hurtled around a truck, and then swerved back towards a precipice and the comforting depths of the Ethiopian plateau.

'Please, sir,' said the driver. 'No lunch, no rest, no dinner.'

I could only imagine he was driving fast to get to the nearest meal. Louis was telling him to go slow and speed up simultaneously, and I happily translated as we lurched over small streams and the car coughed and collapsed by the side of the road.

We started up again and then, at one traumatic moment, another Land Cruiser zipped past us on the unsurfaced road, at a clip that would have qualified it for attention in a NASCAR rally. Minutes later we met it again, in a ditch, its passengers sitting dazed in the front seat.

'No lunch,' cried the driver. 'No breakfast, no lunch, no rest.'

'No hope,' said Louis, and I translated this into warm pleasantries to our guide.

Occasionally, in the midst of emptiness, our leader would see a man he had served with in the military. The car would stop, and pregnant reminiscences would be exchanged. Louis had taken to closing his eyes, as if to make it all go away, and burying his head in Richard Price's novel of gangland violence, *Clockers*. The driver spoke of his war experiences with a nostalgia growing by the minute.

In time, near-dead, we approached a hotel where Louis and the driver with whom he had long since stopped speaking were able to go their separate ways: the driver back to his much-missed home, Louis to the horror of spending less to enjoy more comfort, with Ethiopian Airlines. I, now permanently brown – a human sand dune with a simultaneous translation machine inside (which could only offer translations from English into English) – was moved to reflect on the beauty of travel.

We travel, I thought – looking fondly at my heroic old friend – for adventure and fun, to get away from the drudgery of our lives at home. We travel to court hardship and face the dangers and excitements that are themselves a kind of vacation and challenge for us. We meet people for whom our presence is nothing but opportunity, to take them out of the sadness and difficulty of their lives. The smiles exchanged on both sides have something of a nervous edge.

I looked again at my friend, the best travelling companion I knew, collapsed in an exhausted heap in one corner of the car, too tired even to argue the 'no breakfast, no lunch' conundrum, and thought how the more horrifying the trip, the more amusing it is in retrospect. But humour, everything, encountered on the road, is just a gateway. It only really moves us if it comes very close indeed to something that looks exactly like its opposite.

UPRIVER
STANLEY STEWART

Stanley Stewart is the author of three travel books: *Old Serpent Nile* chronicles a journey from the mouth to the source of the White Nile; *Frontiers of Heaven* records his travels in China along the Silk Road; and *In the Empire of Genghis Khan* is an account of a 1000-mile ride across Mongolia. The last two books both won the Thomas Cook/*Daily Telegraph* Travel Book award in the UK, and have been translated into a dozen languages. When not travelling, Stanley divides his time between Dorset and Rome.

IN BORNEO THERE WERE only two destinations: upriver and down.

Downriver were the sorry towns of Chinese shop-houses, the shuttered government offices and the anxious people of the coast. Upriver was the interior, a world of forests and fat brown streams, of head-hunters and disappointed missionaries, of blowpipes and all-night raves in longhouses decorated with human skulls. Upriver took you to places the roads couldn't reach. It was not merely a destination. In Borneo it was what people were: *hulu* – upriver.

I was feeling kind of *hulu* myself. Perhaps I had been travelling for too long. I wanted some place untroubled by arrivals and departures. I had the notion that upriver might offer stillness, some kind of permanence, after the transient feeling of the towns. Perhaps I toyed with ideas of innocence. I was soon aware that such perceptions were not widely shared in the towns where people tended to think of upriver as a barbarian darkness. Yet they did their best to reassure me. They said the missionaries had done a great deal to persuade the upriver tribes to give up the old habit of decapitating the house guests.

Down at the dock the river clawed at the rotting pylons. The boats looked like aeroplane fuselages that had lost their wings in some nasty incident. Inside the passengers sat in rows of broken seats, mesmerised by the onboard entertainment, a relentless diet of kung fu videos. I took my place between an enormous bald Iban in the terminal stages of emphysema and a boy with a lapful of roosters. A cloud of diesel fumes signalled our departure.

We swung upriver through wide river bends. The water was the colour of wet clay, its swollen surface disturbed by sinister eddies and half-submerged logs. Dark forest pressed down to the water's edge. From time to time the trees parted to reveal the longhouses of the Kayan and the Kenyah tribes. They looked like elongated Appalachian shacks, elevated on stilts, built of timber off-cuts, thatch and corrugated metal. Each longhouse was a communal village of many families, all sharing the same roof, the same verandah and the same problems with noisy neighbours.

Then the trees closed again, and the river was swamped with green reflections. Above us was a wilderness of clouds. As the afternoon wore on, the clouds sank into the treetops, and a melancholy rain came on, pockmarking the smooth surface of the water.

I stayed the night at Long Panai. It wasn't a scheduled stop. The fuselage made a slow fly-past, and I leapt ashore with a triple jump that would have astonished my old gym teacher. Long Panai was a substantial place; the longhouse ran along the riverbank for a quarter of a mile and contained 120 families. People sat outside on the covered verandah sifting rice and gossip. The young people looked like sober suburban kids, with their baseball caps turned backwards, while their parents looked like New Age freaks: a confusion of wild tattoos, pierced body parts, dangling ear lobes, patchwork clothing and funny-looking cigarettes.

I was staying with Thomas, who was a minor royal. His reception room was the model of aristocratic taste, imported from downriver: furnished with purple arm chairs and a lime-green sofa encased in plastic. On the walls, among the ceremonial swords, the hornbill beaks, and the stretched skin of a flying squirrel, was a painting of Jesus and a picture of Bon Jovi torn from a magazine. Jesus and Bon Jovi were both very big in Sarawak.

Both of Thomas' grandfathers had been chiefs, though on opposite sides of a tribal war. His parents' marriage had been part of the peace treaty. Through Thomas' childhood political tensions had masqueraded as domestic strife.

'The old religion gave my family many powers,' Thomas was saying. He was a slow, thoughtful man with a stretched shiny face. 'It was a big responsibility. My paternal grandfather, for instance, could cure the sick by spitting on them. Also he was bulletproof.'

I said it was a wonder they had taken up Christianity when they already had such a useful faith.

'Who needs bulletproofing these days?' he said. 'Like you, we

want to be in Paradise with the Holy Ghost. We want Eternal Life.'
After dinner – a rabbit – we sat outside on the verandah, drinking
bowls of *tuak*, a homemade rice wine with a donkey's kick. Liana
vines, climbing the stilts beneath the longhouse, curled round our
feet. The evening was spread out across the surface of the river.
From the depths of the forest at our backs came a discourse of
animal shrieks. An old branch fell from a tree near the house with
an echoing crash.

'We are rotting here,' Thomas sighed. 'Nothing survives in
these forests. The damp, the termites, the vegetation, they over-
whelm everything. If we fell asleep on these chairs, vines would
be climbing our legs when we woke in the morning.'

Night fell, and the fireflies began to dance.

'When I was young I longed for life downriver. I felt claustro-
phobic here. I wanted someplace with possibilities. Here nothing
changes.'

A chorus of frogs rose from the reed-beds below the house.
Beyond, the river was a sheet of polished blackness, its movement
invisible.

'What do you hope to find in Sarawak?' he asked.

I mumbled something about the drama of the river and virgin
forests. I would have felt foolish talking to him about stillness, the
quality he longed to escape.

'There is nothing here. Only trees and more trees. It is all the
same. There is nowhere to go.'

The next morning I found a boatman with a *prau*, a dugout
canoe, to take me further upriver. After an hour or so on the river
we turned into a tributary where the narrow stream was cluttered
with fallen trees. Hornbills shrieked from the forest canopy. The
forest trailed leafy fingers in the current, and we slipped through
cool chambers of shade beneath the strangler figs. An escarpment
reared on our right, packed with giant hardwoods.

In the early afternoon an Iban longhouse, surrounded by black
pigs and stands of maize, appeared on the left bank of the river. It
was a ramshackle affair elevated on a rickety wilderness of stilts.

Laundry and children dangled from the railings. The chief was away in the fields and we were received by his mother, a tiny octogenarian. Her lips and teeth were crimson with betel nut. Blue tattoos swarmed up her arms and across her bare breasts, and her elongated ear lobes hung down to her shoulders. She served us *tuak* for afternoon tea. It had a faint taste of sticking plasters. Sitting in the front parlour on straw mats, I checked the rafters for skulls, and was disappointed to find there weren't any.

With the boatman as translator, I asked about head-hunting. The woman was old enough to remember its heyday.

'The heads protected us,' she said, her gaze lingering on my cranium as she shifted a vast wad of betel nut from one side of her mouth to the other. 'They made the longhouse safe.'

In the old days, after a head-hunting expedition, the heads were skinned and smoked over a fire before being hung from the rafters in rattan nets. Properly appeased and respected, the heads brought blessings to the longhouse, from warding off evil spirits to producing rain. The magical powers of the heads waned with time so fresh goods were always in demand. Without fresh heads, the old woman said, longhouses are vulnerable. Now we have nothing to protect us.

In the evening we partied. After a rather murky dinner of fish and rice, more *tuak* was produced, and we moved outside to the passageway that acted as the village square. The neighbours began to gather. Music was provided by an erratic cassette player. After a few drinks the dancing began. Young girls arrived wearing sarongs and straw bonnets decorated with hornbill feathers. They turned slowly on the balls of their feet, gesturing with their long-fingered hands.

I asked if it was a dance of courtship. 'A war dance,' the chief cried merrily, throwing back another bowl of *tuak*. The chief was everything his mother was not: big, boisterous and coarse. As the drinking progressed, the entertainment grew a little ragged. A barrel-shaped man in a torn sarong sang 'Oh God Our Help in Ages Past'. He made it sound like a drinking song.

The chief's mother, a stickler for cultural traditions, was unimpressed with such innovation. She disappeared for a time, and when she returned she was wearing a blue silk gown. She had tied her hair in a bun and put kohl around her eyes. The girls and the men fell away and the old woman took centre stage. She danced exquisitely. Her face had the quality of a mask, austere and aloof, while her long delicate hands were full of expression. She was the Margot Fonteyn of Sarawak. Her performance was the highlight of the evening.

Or so, naively, I thought. In fact the entertainment thus far was merely a prelude to the star turn: me. On the wrong side of my tenth bowl of *tuak* I suddenly noticed that the assembled Ibans were waving at me. Closer inspection revealed they were waving me to my feet.

I demurred, but it was too late. A press gang of young women was bearing down on me. Someone put a straw bonnet on my head. Strong arms were lifting me. Through a veil of hornbill feathers, I suddenly found myself standing before the entire longhouse: a sea of expectant upturned faces. 'Make the Dance of England,' bellowed the chief.

In a *tuak*-inspired moment, I decided against such narrow nationalism and opted instead for the Dance of Europe. It seemed to offer more scope.

I began with the flamenco, a stirring rendition of heel-clicking and finger-snapping. I moved on to a Bohemian polka, interspersing this with bits of an Alpine jig of my own invention. Dizziness cut short the Irish reel and I passed groggily on to a high-kicking Cossack number which I ascribed to the Poles. When I tried a bit of Morris dancing, it came out like a storm troopers' rally.

My audience went wild. They held their sides and hooted. They beat the ground and howled. Even the chief's mother was amused. She clung to a post, dabbing at her eyes.

My performance marked the end of the evening, for which I was grateful. I felt I had been dancing on the *Titanic*. The longhouse seemed to be pitching in heavy seas. I made my way to a corner of the chief's front parlour and was asleep before I had finished unrolling my mat. At dawn I was awoken by the routine longhouse cacophony: crowing roosters, howling dogs and people quarrelling over breakfast five households away.

My performance of the previous evening had earned me a reputation as a comic turn. Crowds now gathered to watch me eat breakfast in the hope that I might do something funny. I was unable to oblige unless a minor bout of retching over the grilled chicken feet counted as fun. Perhaps understandably, my audience seemed to believe it did.

We pressed onwards, following the trail of rivers further into the interior. Herons patrolled the banks, lifting their feet primly from the water with each step. Brilliant kingfishers, blue and orange, flashed among the overhanging boughs. A monitor lizard, as still and gnarled as driftwood, watched us from a sandbank. A tribe of gibbons passed through the treetops on our right, hooting as they went. Fish eagles rose from their perches at our approach, and flew away upriver, disappearing around the bend ahead. Through that whole afternoon, as we bore upriver, we were preceded by eagles.

In the early evening we came to the last longhouse on the river. Women were washing in the shallows, and their voices and soft laughter drifted across the water. We moored the canoe and followed them up a mud path. The stairway, leading up to the longhouse platform, was a log carved in the form of a woman. Steps had been notched up the sides of her thighs and ribs. A few people sat outside their doors in the wide passageway that ran the length of the house. Tiny oil lamps burned at their feet, throwing tall shadows across the walls above their heads.

In the twilight fireflies swooned above the water like errant stars, and the pigs snuffled beneath the house.

I called in on the headman, and fell into another discussion about religion. Like Thomas, he was an enthusiast for Christianity. It might have knocked head-hunting on the head, but in other respects he reckoned it was a good thing. His chief worry was backsliders. The Baptists used to operate in these regions, he explained, but the pastor, who was based on the coast, was no longer able to make the journey upriver. In the absence of the Baptists, things were getting out of hand, and the chief hoped the Anglicans might take an interest.

'Harvest festival is a bad time for backsliding,' the chief said. 'So much drinking and playing with the girls. The girls become so frisky, and the boys get too virile.'

I tried to look disapproving. I had heard about the harvest festivals. It was a time of carousing and licentiousness. In the party atmosphere, women strapped large phalluses round their waist, and taunted their menfolk. I cursed myself for travelling at the wrong season.

'I am thinking the Anglicans could sort us out once and for all,' he said. 'Do you know any Anglicans?'

'A few,' I said. 'Not overly virile.'

'I think it is time for the Anglicans.'

'I shall mention it to them. It sounds like an Anglican kind of thing.'

In the morning the longhouse was wrapped in a cloud, and the river was a tunnel of mist beneath dripping branches. After breakfast I set off for a walk through the forests. Among a tangle of orchids, I came upon the tomb of a local dignitary. In the riot of vegetation it looked like a garden shed overwhelmed by its garden. The boatman explained that the former chief had been a key figure in the War of the Penises, a notorious altercation that had neighbouring tribes trading insults to one another's manhood.

The great man had been buried with his belongings, which were littered about the sarcophagus inside the shed: a few clothes, an old wireless, a favourite rattan chair, some pillows, his shield and two swords. Thirty years had made them look like garden shed junk, rusty, cobwebbed, moth-eaten and mouldy. In another 30 years, they would be jungle. I thought of Thomas: nothing survives in these forests.

We walked on, cutting back towards the river where a canoe

from the longhouse was waiting. Two boatmen poled me upriver over shallow rapids. Their shins were tattooed with fish hooks, a talisman for fisherman's luck. The longhouses all lay behind us now. The river narrowed to a green aisle beneath the leafy vaults of the forest. Giant hardwoods rose from beds of tiny unfurled ferns. The water was clear as air, running over smooth amber boulders. A long curve brought us to a waterfall. Beyond, the river was too shallow for boats. This place, miles above the last longhouse, was as far upriver as men ever came.

We drew the boat onto the sand bank and the boatmen made a fire and cooked lunch: chicken flavoured with lemon grass and ginger, baked inside bamboo. I swam in the sheltered pool beneath the waterfall. The forest tilted above me, overhanging the water, trailing vines like long stout ropes. The air was full of butterflies, iridescent green and lemon yellow. The boatmen sharpened their swords on the rocks, smoked palm-leaf roll-ups and watched the tree tops, cradling their blowpipes. Some sweet stillness was suspended on the liquid notes of birds.

I asked the boatmen the name of this place. They shrugged. It has no name, they said.

Eden, it occurred to me, must have been like this: a river, a sandbank, dappled sunlight, birdsong, the close embrace of forests. It was a virginal world. There was nothing to disturb this place. Only ourselves.

SOMETHING APPROACHING ENLIGHTENMENT

ROLF POTTS

Rolf Potts is the author of *Vagabonding: An Uncommon Guide to the Art of Long-Term World Travel* and *Marco Polo Didn't Go There: Stories and Revelations From One Decade as a Postmodern Travel Writer*. His work has appeared in venues such as *National Geographic Traveler,* the *New York Times Magazine,* the Best American Travel Writing series, the Travel Channel, and numerous Lonely Planet anthologies. Though he keeps no permanent address, he tends to linger in Thailand, Egypt, rural Kansas and France, where he runs a summertime creative writing workshop at the Paris American Academy. His online home is www .rolfpotts.com.

FOR WEEKS AFTER returning from my ill-fated journey to the Indian Himalayan village of Kaza, I had difficulty explaining to people why I'd wanted to go there in the first place. Sometimes I'd claim it had something to do with the Dalai Lama – though someone would always point out, correctly, that the Dalai Lama lived in the Tibetan exile capital at Dharamsala, not in some obscure mountain outpost several days in the other direction.

I had no easy answer to this seeming discrepancy. Granted, the Dalai Lama was reputed to travel to Kaza once each summer – but I'd gone there in the winter. And while rumour had it that the Dalai Lama planned to spend his twilight years in a monastery just up the valley from Kaza, the famous Tibetan holy man was nowhere near retirement at the time of my visit. In the end, I suppose my decision to gain an understanding of the Dalai Lama by going where he didn't live was grounded in a vague fear of disappointment – a fear that (as with other religious destinations I'd visited in India, such as Varanasi and Rishikesh) Dharamsala had become so popular with other Western travellers that any spiritual epiphanies I found there would feel forced and generic.

By contrast, the Indo-Tibetan village of Kaza was the most remote Himalayan destination I could reach by road in late winter. There, in the cobbled alleyways of an ancient and windswept Buddhist village, I imagined I might find a more authentic vision of what the Dalai Lama represented. Far from the well-worn lanes of Dharamsala, I hoped I might better be able to discover something approaching enlightenment.

Thus, from the northern Indian hub city of Shimla, I'd walked to the far end of the bus terminal – past the backpack-toting crowds of Westerners headed to Dharamsala – and boarded the first in a series of buses that would take me to my far-flung Himalayan Shangri-La.

While still within the fog of my initial inspiration, it was fairly easy to rationalise a three-day bus ride through the remote Himalayas. Once I was actually en route to Kaza, however, I immediately

31

realised that my whimsical pilgrimage could very well get me killed. The copy of the *Hindustan Times* that I'd bought in Shimla, for instance, devoted an entire front-page story to grisly mountain bus crashes. 'At least 40 people were killed when a bus plunged into a tributary of the Ravi River yesterday evening,' the article read. 'Earlier in the day, eight people died and thirteen were injured when a truck carrying them fell into a gorge 35 kilometres from Manali.'

The Indian highway signs were not much more encouraging. In lieu of shoulders or guardrails, dangerous curves on the mountain featured boulders with white-painted slogans that read 'O God help us!' or 'Be safe: use your horn'. I kept staring out at the river valley 300 metres below and imagining our driver cheerily honking the horn as we all plummeted to certain death.

The most alarming part of the Himalayan bus ride, however, was the road itself, which seemed to be buried under massive mudslides at 80-kilometre intervals. Indeed, every couple of hours, our bus driver would screech to a halt and I'd peer out the window to see what had formerly been the road lying in a crumpled crust 20 metres down the mountain. Invariably, several dozen Indian highway workers would be making a frenzied effort to carve a makeshift dirt track into the flank of the mud wall in front of us. My fellow passengers would disembark and smoke cigarettes at the edge of the cliff, watching disinterestedly until the labourers gave a shout and our bus driver would rumble across the improvised mud road. Along with the other passengers, I'd then follow on foot at a safe distance, climbing back into the bus once the normal highway resumed. My main solace amidst all this was the promise of Kaza and the serene Buddhist environs that hopefully awaited me there.

After two days of nonstop travel, I'd made it deep into the Tibetan border region before the transmission dropped out of the bottom of my bus near a town called Pooh. Folks in Pooh informed me that there were no more onward buses that day, but I might be able to find transportation out of Kob, 10 kilometres further up the road. Feeling optimistic in the early-afternoon sunshine, I set off for Kob on foot.

In retrospect, the early hours of my hike to Kob were the happiest of my entire Himalayan sojourn. Outside of Pooh, the altitude snaked up to above 3500 metres, and the hand-planted cherry trees along the roadside had just begun to sprout pink blossoms. Before long, though, I was trudging into a massive canyon of grey rock and the highway was reduced to a narrow slot dynamited out of the side of the cliff. The Spiti River was barely visible below, but I knew it was the same river that roared down from Kaza – a place where I envisioned cool air, welcoming locals and the soft tinkling of monastery bells.

Unfortunately, the transit town of Kob never materialised, even after four hours of hiking. I trudged an additional hour in the dark before I spied an abandoned blockhouse at the side of the road. Figuring it was as good a place as any to bivouac, I pulled on several layers of warm clothing, curled up on the dirt floor, and – exhausted – fell asleep. When I woke up, my watch told me it was just past seven o'clock. Encouraged to have had a full night's sleep, I walked outside to catch the sunrise.

I must have stared at the darkened eastern horizon for half an hour before I re-checked my watch and noticed the small 'PM' over the time-code.

Nervous about the gathering mountain cold, I began a search for firewood – but all I could find was the old wooden block-house door, which had long since fallen off its hinges. When repeated attempts to smash the door with rocks resulted in nary a dent, I tried tossing it into the air and breaking it over the large roadside boulders.

I had been tossing the door onto the boulders without success for about 15 minutes before I realised I was being watched by half a dozen bewildered-looking Indian soldiers. Not knowing what else to do, I put my hands above my head. One of the soldiers grabbed my backpack and the others marched me half a mile up the road to their transport truck, where I met a no-nonsense lieutenant who (apart from the beard, turban and Punjabi accent) looked somewhat like the movie star Vin Diesel.

'My soldiers tell me you were taking photographs,' he said. 'Is this true?'

'No,' I told him. 'I was trying to smash up a door.'

Lieutenant Diesel shot me a suspicious look. 'This is a dangerous border, and it's not for tourists. Why did you bring a door?'

After a witheringly absurd 10-minute interrogation about my motives for trying to destroy a door in total darkness along the Indian–Chinese border, Lieutenant Diesel consented to drive me back to his army base near Pooh. There, I was allowed to sleep on a bench in a small administrative office. 'If anybody asks,' the lieutenant told me gravely, 'tell them you were taking photographs.'

The following day, I hitched a ride on a troop transport to the village of Yangthang, where I was finally able to catch a bus that took me over a final stretch of highway switchbacks and road washouts to my mountain-top destination. As I stumbled out of the bus at the Kaza depot, I marvelled at the stark simplicity of the town, which consisted of whitewashed houses and small storefronts spread along a scree-strewn basin. Two monasteries were perched on the surrounding hillsides, and I noticed with delight that the stones along the walkway had been carved with Buddhist prayers. The place looked like a picture postcard of Tibetan authenticity.

When I walked into the centre of town, however, I was disappointed to find that – save for wandering packs of stray dogs – Kaza was largely deserted. All the guesthouses were shuttered for the winter, and the few ethnic Tibetan residents I passed on the street couldn't understand my English queries. The only person who took an interest in me was a chubby, balding man at the government-housing complex, who introduced himself as Mr Singh.

'Come and drink with us!' he hollered happily. 'Today we cele-brate the Holi festival. It is very important to Hindus.' I politely declined Mr Singh's offer, explaining that I had come to Kaza to experience Buddhist culture.

Since the local monasteries were as empty and gated as the hotels, however, I was quickly running out of options. Stopping to check my guidebook, I noticed that Ki Gompa, a historically isolated thousand-year-old monastery, was just 14 kilometres from Kaza via a mountain trail. With the realisation that all my travails up to that point might really just be hints of fate leading me to the halls of Ki Gompa, I shouldered my pack and headed to the footpath on the edge of town.

As I walked, I felt a slight twinge of pity for all the travellers who made their way to Dharamsala seeking the Dalai Lama, only to wind up in guesthouses and internet cafes full of travellers from Berkeley and Birmingham and Tel Aviv. By contrast, I reckoned my final push to Ki Gompa would transcend such tourist banality and lead me into the true heart of Tibetan spirituality.

Fewer than 200 metres up the mountain – and with these happy delusions still floating in my head – a giant mastiff charged out from behind a rock, bared his teeth and tore off my right trouser leg at the knee. Spooked, I ran all the way back down into Kaza, blood oozing into my socks. Since I didn't know of any other options, I jogged over to the government-housing complex.

'You have come back to celebrate Holi!' Mr Singh exclaimed upon seeing me.

'Actually, a dog bit me and I need some first aid.' I pointed at my bleeding wound.

With the formal air of a person who is doing his best to feign sobriety, Mr Singh shook my hand in sympathy and led me to a small cinderblock hospital just up the road. One tetanus shot and one roll of gauze later, I was back in the housing complex, being introduced to Mr Singh's colleagues – Mr Gupta, who was as bald and chubby as Mr Singh, and Mr Kumar, a thin middle-aged man with hunched shoulders and owlish eyeglasses. Mr Singh merrily explained that they were all road engineers from the Delhi area, and that they hated living in Kaza. 'This is an ugly place,' he said, 'and it is filled with country people who have no culture or sophistication.'

Mr Gupta proposed they give me a Holi blessing, so I followed them into Mr Kumar's room, which, with its stovepipe oven, peeling wallpaper and magazine photos of Bollywood starlets, looked like a cross between a college dorm and a miner's cabin. Three bottles of Director's Special whisky sat empty on the top of a dresser. Mr Gupta produced a jar of chalky red pigment and smeared a *tikka* mark on my forehead, while Mr Singh opened a fresh bottle of Director's Special and poured me a glass.

'So why do Hindus celebrate Holi?' I asked.

'It comes from a story in our ancient book, the *Mahabharata*,' Mr Singh slurred. 'Exactly one million years ago there was a goddess who tortured her brother to death. So now we celebrate.'

'It is a very enjoyable holiday', Mr Gupta added.

'What do you do when you celebrate Holi?'

'Sometimes we throw buckets of coloured water at our friends or at strangers. But today, since you are our guest, we will watch movies of the colour blue.' Mr Singh shot me a conspiratorial look. 'Of course, you know which movies I mean.'

'I don't think so,' I said. 'Are they movies about the *Mahabharata*?'

'No, these movies are much more interesting.' Mr Singh gestured to Mr Kumar, who popped a videotape into the VCR. Throbbing synthesiser music crackled out of the TV speaker, and a fuzzy image shuddered onto the screen. The movie had such poor picture quality that I could barely tell what was going on – though it appeared to be the writhing of two or more naked bodies. Presently, the synthesiser music was offset by slurping, slapping and moaning noises. 'Oh yeah,' a voice from the TV said. 'Ride me harder!'

I shot Mr Singh a quizzical look, and he giggled boyishly. 'Mr Kumar wants to know why that man has such a long penis,' he said.

'Long and fat,' Mr Gupta said.

I looked back at the TV, but still couldn't make out a clear image. Apparently, these men had rewound and fast-forwarded the movie so many times that it had deteriorated into jumbled images of static and fuzz. Only the soundtrack remained.

Assuming it was a fairly standard porno movie, I considered my answer. 'I guess it's part of the job qualification,' I said. 'Men in blue movies need to have big penises, just like men who build roads need to have engineering degrees.'

Mr Singh translated this for Mr Kumar; the men nodded seriously.

'What about this,' Mr Singh said, gesturing at the screen. 'Is this normal for married men in America?'

I squinted at the TV, but couldn't make out what was going on. 'Is what normal?'

'To have two women licking one man's penis,' Mr Gupta said.

'Only one of them is his wife', Mr Singh clarified, 'and the other woman brought them a pizza on her motorcycle.'

'Oh my God!' the TV crackled. 'Don't stop.'

'Listen,' I said, 'these kinds of movies are just fantasies. You can't assume they represent anything about normal American life. I mean, what if everyone thought life in India was exactly like a Bollywood musical?'

'But Bollywood movies are very accurate!' Mr Singh exclaimed. 'They show many good things about India.'

'But they don't represent normal Indian life,' I said. 'I mean, do you and Mr Gupta and Mr Kumar break into song and dance every day at work?'

'I like to sing and dance,' Mr Gupta offered.

'That's right,' the TV interjected. 'Give it to me, you big stud!'

Before the conversation could deteriorate any further, there was a knock on the door and a teenage boy walked in to serve us

37

bowls of dhal. 'This is Vikram,' Mr Gupta said. 'He is a student of English.'

'He will look at this movie, and then he will want to run off for hand practice,' Mr Singh giggled, making a wanking motion.

Vikram gave me a sympathetic look as he handed me the dhal. 'These guys are hammered,' he whispered. 'Just let me know if they start to bother you.'

Ten minutes later, I caught up with Vikram in the housing-compound kitchen. 'Look,' I told him, 'I travelled for three days on some of the worst roads I've seen in my life just to get to Kaza. I have nothing against Holi or Hindus, but I was hoping to meet some Tibetans here. Do you know of any way I can stay at one of the Buddhist monasteries?'

'You've come here at the end of winter,' he said, 'and only a handful of trucks and buses have made it through since November. The monasteries are running low on food, and the guesthouses won't want to turn on their generators for just one person. You should stay the night in Mr Kumar's room. It's pretty comfortable.'

'But isn't there any way to meet some Buddhists while I'm in Kaza?'

Vikram shrugged. 'Maybe, but people stay indoors during this time. And they don't know much English. You'd probably get bored if you don't speak any Tibetan. You should come back in June or July. That's the best time for tourists.'

For some reason, the word 'tourists' triggered an instant and vivid fantasy. I imagined myself off in the streets of Dharamsala – eating muesli, flirting with Norwegian backpacker girls, sending emails to friends back in the States and swapping Dalai Lama–sighting stories with star-struck Canadians. Suddenly, this scenario didn't seem so bad at all.

Resigned to my fate, however, I returned to Mr Kumar's room. There, as we fast-forwarded through several more scenes from the movie (which appeared to be about a team of unusually libidinous pizza delivery women), I served as an informal ambassador of American marginalia.

'Yes,' I told them, 'I'm pretty sure Viagra works. No, I haven't tried it. Yes, I'm aware that Bill Clinton and Monica Lewinsky had sexual relations. No, I don't think they still keep in touch. Actually, I don't think they were ever in love to begin with. Yes, there are many famous black Americans named Michael. Yes, I know all about Michael Jackson's career. No, I don't think that would make Michael Jordan want to get plastic surgery.'

Eventually Mr Singh and Mr Gupta staggered off to bed, and I fell asleep on Mr Kumar's floor, next to the woodstove. A little after midnight, I awakened to see the stoop-shouldered Indian sitting on the edge of his bed, intently watching the snowy image of a naked man and woman engaged in a sexual act that was technically outlawed in numerous states and countries.

Seeing that I was awake, Mr Kumar grinned over at me and, with a knowing wobble of his head, said, 'Back-door entry!'

This was the only English I ever heard him speak.

Sometime before sunrise, Vikram came into the room and shook me awake. 'I know of a fuel truck that is leaving in 10 minutes. It can take you as far as Pooh, and you can catch a normal bus from there.' He paused for a moment. 'Or, if you want to stay in Kaza longer, the regular bus leaves next week.'

Two minutes later, I was fully packed and sprinting for the fuel truck.

The ensuing three days were not too eventful. Though the muddy Himalayan highway was just as precarious as it had been on my inbound journey, I didn't let it get to me; I merely looked forward to getting back to the well-worn grooves of the tourist trail. As a new series of buses rattled me back down towards Shimla, I stared out at the steep mountain canyons with Zen-like patience.

I had indeed, it seemed, achieved something approaching enlightenment.

THE END OF THE ROAD
BILL FINK

Bill Fink somehow escaped his Thai predicament despite the brief arrest of his copilot, and a near mob lynching. Currently based in San Francisco, Bill lives on the high adventure and low pay of freelance travel writing and photography. He writes regularly for the *San Francisco Chronicle* and other newspapers, magazines, websites and guidebooks. You can read his equally inept journey up Mt Fuji in Lonely Planet's *By the Seat of My Pants* anthology, and see his other adventures at www.billfinktravels.com.

WE LOST THE SIDE-VIEW MIRRORS somewhere outside Nakhon Ratchasima. They shattered when Ben steered our jeep too close to the thick Thai jungle choking the roadside. The gas gauge and speedometer went at Bua Yai, the transmission failed near Khon Kaen, and we snapped the driveshaft 12 long miles from Udon Thani. Only the broken driveshaft really slowed us down, adding a day's delay in our quest to see the Real Thailand.

On winter break from a study abroad program in Japan, Ben and I had decided we would skip the typical backpacker trip to the tropical Thai party islands of Koh Samui and Phuket. And we certainly weren't going to go on one of those packaged air-con bus tours of the country, sharing our seats with grey-haired old ladies from Peoria and honeymooning Japanese couples in matching sweatsuits.

No, our plan was to discover the true Thailand by driving straight to the middle of nowhere. We felt the further we left the beaten path, the better chance we'd have to meet the locals, experience the culture, and become one with the people. We rented a jeep to help us navigate the harsh backroads terrain. But we had to give up on the idea of blending with the locals, because the only jeep we were able to rent had bright yellow flames painted on the side, big chrome bumpers and a decal that said 'Pattaya Party Cruiser' on the hood. Plus, we were two long-haired, bearded white guys who couldn't speak a word of Thai, and had a bit of trouble remembering which side of the road we were supposed to drive on.

But we were as friendly as we were filthy, and we figured a little sincerity would go a long way towards bonding with the locals. At the start of our trip we had decent luck befriending Thai people, especially as we revitalised village economies with all the money we were spending on jeep repairs. But as we headed to the hills of the northeast, people became a little less open and a little more cautious about engaging with us. The area at the intersection of Thailand, Myanmar and Laos, infamously known as the Golden

Triangle, had been a vortex of the opium trade, cross-border battles, tribal insurgencies, and general mayhem for generations. In the months before our arrival, a military coup in Myanmar had resulted in the slaughter of protesters, closing of borders, and rebel fighters using the Thai countryside as a hiding ground. The Laos–Thailand border was also closed, due to a simmering border dispute between the two countries that had been sparking small military skirmishes.

This information was very revealing when we learned it a month later, after our return to Japan. But as we drove into the Triangle, we were blissfully unaware of why Thai troops manned roadblocks at every mountain pass, and why they looked at us like we were raging lunatics. We figured it was business as usual as they searched all our gear for guns, drugs or some other clue as to why we were driving through the middle of nowhere. The troops were friendly enough, but as the day progressed we noticed bottles of Singha Beer and Mekhong Whisky strewn around the barricades, and the soldiers getting a little more pushy with their searches, waving their M-16s around a bit too recklessly.

To avoid the roadblocks, we followed smaller dirt roads into the hills. Low on gas (or at least we thought so, not having a working gauge) and lost in the mountains, we crisscrossed rocky paths looking for any sort of town for a fill-up. As we crested a hill, I spotted a village tucked into the forest. It consisted of about a dozen tidy but faded wood houses surrounding several larger two-storey structures that looked like stores. Children played in the hard-packed dirt of the central square, kicking around a *tákrâw* wicker ball, while elders sat in the shade on the porch of the main store, hiding from the late afternoon heat.

The villagers' heads rose and turned in unison as our jeep rumbled downhill towards town. By the time we had pulled into the square, every last man, woman and child had fled. They dove into doorways, ducked behind buildings, or flat out ran for the hills.

Ben and I sat in the idling jeep, smiles frozen on our faces, hands not even finished with our hello waves.

'What'd we do?' I asked Ben.

'Oh, we're idiots. They don't wave here, they do that *wâi* thing, you know, hands together in prayer, close to the chest, fingers near chin, like this.' Ben demonstrated, and sat in the driver's seat like a bearded Buddha with his *wâi* ready to welcome the villagers back to their own town.

'Or maybe we should turn off the stereo; they might not like Hendrix,' I added, clicking off the cassette deck along with the ignition.

We sat silently for 10 minutes, but still no townspeople appeared. Ben's *wâi* drooped as the sun beat down on our open-topped jeep. Here we were, parked smack dab in the centre of a town in the middle of Thailand, and we couldn't have been further from connecting with the spirit of the country. We were just two goofs in a jeep who might as well have been in a Wal-Mart parking lot.

A door creaked open in the wooden building across the street from us. A pot-bellied middle-aged Thai man emerged. He straightened his wire-rim glasses, buttoned his collared shirt, frowning as he patted down the creases, adding a couple of taps to his stomach. He turned his face towards us, smiled and shouted, 'Friend!'

We smiled, gave him a *wâi*, and hopped down from the jeep, ready to bond.

'Hello,' said Ben. '*Sawat di krap*,' he added.

'Friend!' shouted the Thai man, still smiling. He extended his hand.

I reached to shake the hand, which he did with vigour. But he didn't let go. He put his other hand on my back, and not so subtly directed me back to the jeep.

'Friend! Peace!' he added, still shouting, as he gripped my hand with renewed intensity.

'He must be the mayor,' Ben guessed. 'Let's ask him where we can find some gas for the jeep.'

We tried to get some information out of our greeter, but couldn't get beyond 'friend' and 'peace', which certainly are two very good words, but weren't going to move the jeep very far. In the background, we noticed a few kids creeping out of the shadows to see what was happening at the Showdown in the Square.

Giving up on English, we pointed to Thai words in our phrasebook, but still couldn't get an answer from Mr Peace. We pointed to our jeep, the cap of the gas tank, and the road out of town. At this, our friend brightened.

'Nan! Nan!' He shouted out the name of the next large town to the east. We figured he probably wasn't offering us Indian flatbread.

'OK, thanks, yes, we know it's up the road a piece, but we need some gas, petrol, *nahm man baehn sin.*' I tried some Thai out of the phrasebook.

He shouted 'Nan!' again, pointed to the east, then escorted us back into the jeep, gesturing to the road ahead.

'I believe we're being run out of town,' Ben said, as he was cordially shoved into the driver's seat. The mayor recoiled slightly as our stereo started along with the motor, but he never lost his smile at the prospect of the two hippies leaving town.

We drove east, meandering on unmarked roads for half an hour before seeing another army roadblock. It was the standard long tree branch, painted red, held across the road by a tattered rope. Sandbags lined a wooden guardhouse; slouching soldiers stood with guns loosely hanging from straps at their shoulders.

'Here we go again,' said Ben. 'Grab another pack of chewing gum for a gift, and see if they'll tell us where a gas station is.'

'Whoa, you think these guys are Special Forces? They're wearing blue uniforms instead of the usual green.' I scanned the soldiers as we slowed to a stop. They gave us the same astonished look that we had been seeing all day. And as usual, they began shouting at us. We smiled, shrugged our shoulders, and pointed at our ragged map to demonstrate we were lost.

'*Arrêtez! Pourquoi vous-venez ici?*' One soldier began yelling at us in French, moving in front of the gate, hand resting on his gun, which had the characteristic forward-angled banana-shaped ammunition clip of an AK-47.

'Wait a minute, what's this guy speaking French for?' I asked. 'Since when do Thai people speak French? And um, he's not carrying the same weapon…or wearing the same uniform…'

'Oh crap, welcome to Laos,' Ben muttered under his breath. In our search for the centre of things, we had driven clear off the edge of the map.

'*Aimez-vous gum?*' Ben smiled and offered a pack of Doublemint to the increasingly agitated Lao soldier. The soldier shouted in a mix of French, Lao and just plain Pissed Off, all the while pointing behind us. We were all too happy to turn around, retreating to the main road where we soon came upon a medium-sized Thai army base, complete with armoured cars and helicopter. Sent away from that camp, we stopped at a roadside stall where we bought two gallons of gas in plastic jugs. When queried for directions, the gas man just said 'Nan' and pointed north.

The light was fading as we bumped along the rutted dirt road, hoping it was the one that would finally lead us to Nan. We drove by miles of sugar cane fields before we reached a surprisingly modern village, with electric lights lining the streets, concrete houses with corrugated tin roofs, perfectly aligned gates in front and…

'Where the hell are all the people?' asked Ben, scanning the streets. 'There's not even a dog. Everyplace we've been has had dogs running around.'

'Weird,' I said. 'It's like *The Martian Chronicles*. You know, the Bradbury story where the Martians created a perfect little town in imitation of what they thought a home town should look like. The Martians gave the foreign visitors a false sense of security before they killed them all in their sleep.'

'Dude, that's not helpful at all.'

'Or wait,' I added, the quiet darkness fuelling my fear, 'this is like one of those Vietnam War resettlement towns – where US soldiers burnt down villages supporting guerrillas and moved the people to a controlled area. This could be the resettled village of some opium-growing rebels who have run back to the hills to continue their fight. That'd be a more realistic explanation, right?'

As an answer, Ben quickly accelerated the jeep out of the brightly lit ghost town.

The narrowing dirt road led us through an expanse of planted fields. In the darkness we couldn't tell if the fields were planted with short sugar cane or tall opium crops.

'Outstanding,' Ben said. 'If we run into someone out here in the dark we're screwed. The drug traffickers are going to shoot us because they'll think we're government agents, the government agents are going to shoot us because they'll think we're drug runners. We better find that town fast.'

'Wait, I think I see light ahead.' I pointed to a glow coming from an area on the other side of a mountain a few miles to the north. 'That has to be Nan.'

'About time.' Ben gunned the motor, then braked the jeep to a skidding halt. I looked at him in confusion, but he just pointed ahead of us. A 30-foot-long wooden bridge crossed a crevice with a river rushing through twenty-five feet below.

'You think this bridge is meant for cars?' I asked. 'It doesn't look like it can hold much more than a mule.' Long flat planks lay irregularly across raw logs stacked crosswise on the bridge supports. Crudely sawed boards created two tracks on either side of the bridge that *might* be meant for the wheels of a car. Or they might be meant for inbound and outbound mule traffic.

'We gotta get to Nan,' Ben said, and edged the jeep onto the first set of planks. One snapped. I stepped one foot out on the running board of the jeep.

'Where you going?' Ben asked.

'If this thing collapses beneath us, I don't want to go down with the jeep.'

Ben laughed, 'Come on, have some faith,' but he slid to

the edge of his seat, steering with his left hand, with his right foot ready to launch him away from the soon-to-be-imploding bridge.

We crept across a couple of feet at a time, wincing each time the bridge snapped, creaked, and moaned beneath us. It sounded like we were driving across a large, sick water buffalo. With 10 feet to go, Ben gunned the jeep, and we flew across to the other side, leaving a chorus of breaking wood behind us. The bridge still stood, but we weren't sure for how much longer.

'Thank God, we made it!' Ben sped the jeep down the still-narrowing dirt road. The brush scraped the sides of the jeep, scratching what was left of our beautiful flaming decals. But the lights ahead became brighter as we approached the hill. Ben cheered as we reached the summit, practically singing, 'Hello Nan, goodbye Killing Fields, we can finally relax!'

We crested the ridge and sat speechless, the only sound the jeep's motor idling in the silent night air. From our vantage point, we could see the road descending into a wide valley fronted by a large forest. We had finally found the source of the light: the forest was on fire.

We had begun our journey with a quest to find cultural enlightenment by going to the middle of nowhere. Instead we found the end of the road: that exact spot where you can't go forward, can't go backward, and really don't want to stay where you are.

JOURNEY TO THE CENTRE OF THE EARTH

ALANA SEMUELS

Born and raised in Boston, Massachusetts, Alana Semuels can't seem to shake her travel bug. While wandering the world from Antigua to Zimbabwe, she's taught English in Greece, worked in a clinic in Botswana and lost her passport in China. Semuels started her journalism career with the *Pittsburgh Post-Gazette,* wrote for the *Boston Globe* in London and is currently a staff writer for the *Los Angeles Times.*

IF YOU FOLLOW THE EQUATOR around the globe, you fly over Borneo and the Democratic Republic of Congo and an expanse of ocean so long it is hard to imagine its distance.

Go overland and you might see a peeling sign by a road telling you that you are standing on the equator, but most countries have better things to do than devote their dollars or francs or rupias to an invisible line dividing the world.

Ecuador is not most countries. Near its capital, Quito, it has devoted a whole museum to Mitad del Mundo, or the middle of the world. If you're picturing a journey to the centre of the earth's core, you'll be disappointed. Instead, the Mitad del Mundo is a granite building topped by a metallic green globe, with yellow lines painted on the ground approximating what the equator might look like, if indeed it could be seen.

I am staring up at the globe, balancing on the yellow line, not quite ready to hop into the southern hemisphere, although I know I am already there. I am in Ecuador to witness the wedding of my childhood friend Leah, who joined the Peace Corps, fell madly in love with Jorge, an Ecuadorian mechanic, and surprised her parents and pretty much everybody else by announcing that they were getting hitched.

The wedding visitors, who are all Jewish and American, are Leah's parents and brother, a few assorted aunts and uncles, my parents who have known her since she was born, and me, born one year after her and certainly not one to go off and marry someone who doesn't speak English and has never left his village. Or at least this is what I tell my parents when they make me promise for the ninth time since breakfast that I will never, ever pull anything like this. The adults hope that I am their secret weapon – I will stride in and Leah will come to her senses and realise that she needs someone who can at least speak English, preferably a Jewish doctor with Red Sox season tickets.

But Leah's destiny was sealed before she even arrived in Ecuador. The rate of marriages between female Peace Corps volunteers and Ecuadorian men is much higher than it is in other places where the organisation sends unsuspecting and unmarried young women, Leah tells me. One of the other volunteers has already married an Ecuadorian teacher, and another has been living for decades with her barefoot children and farmer husband in a small village without so much as a TV set to link her to the English-speaking world. It must be something in the water, I think, and can understand why my parents keep checking to make sure I haven't found an Ecuadorian man myself.

Signs at the site say that while standing on the equator, you move at a pace of 1.667 kilometres per hour, which is faster than you are moving anywhere else on the globe. I believe it. My head is spinning and it feels like the earth has started to speed its rotation, because Leah is getting married in Ecuador and I can't even communicate with her groom. She has arranged our trip to the middle of the earth perhaps as a subtle reminder that we Americans are not only on a different continent but also in a different hemisphere. I can only focus on the sobering fact that everyone we pass on the street may soon be Leah's relative by marriage.

My first meeting with Jorge is not smooth. My Spanish is rusty, his English vocabulary is limited to a handful of words, and neither of us can think of anything to say in our shared smattering of phrases.

'How are you?' I ask in Spanish.

'Fine,' he replies. He launches into a question, which I pretend to understand.

'Yes,' I answer. 'It is very hot.'

He is clearly puzzled. Wrong answer, I think. I try again.

'I like to dance,' I say, and then, as my grand finale, I finish up with the last phrase I can remember in my jet lag-induced panic. I try to wish him congratulations on his engagement. '*Feliz Navidad.*'

He nods, pleased. Only later do I remember that this means Merry Christmas.

We pile into two white vans and head to Latacunga, where the wedding will take place. The wedding is here because it is easy to reach from Quito and because the groom's family lives here, but not because it is one of Ecuador's top 10 tourist destinations. The Best of Ecuador website sums up Latacunga pretty well: 'This is not an invigorating town'. It's muddy and built of concrete, and our hotel/motel is on the highway leading out of the city. Latacunga's highlights are two volcanoes in the far distance that are spewing smoke. I can see Leah's mother estimate their distance, hoping they might explode, scattering the guests like ashes to their far corners of the world.

The next morning, we are determined to tour at least part of the southern hemisphere before the evening wedding, and take off again in our two dirty white vans to explore the villages outside of Latacunga. We drive along a winding road full of potholes while a nasty wind stirs up the pebbles on the ground.

I am not sure who I feel more sorry for – the driver or myself. He is stuck navigating country roads with a van full of Americans who have funny accents and a deep determination to stop and see everything – and I mean everything – we pass.

'Look at the mountains. Have you ever seen mountains like that?' my mother begins. 'Let's stop and take a picture.'

'Signs in Spanish! I wonder what they say,' delights the bride's aunt. 'Stop – we need to take a picture.'

'Look at the poor woman with her children and a goat! Are they naked? She only has one eye! How charming,' says aunt number two. 'Let's take a picture.'

We stop at every farm and village we see, buying trinkets and wandering around the chilly landscape. We drift into churches and food stores, through empty courtyards, and snap photos of toothless men drinking cola out of glass bottles with straws.

I feel sure that we are on the other side of the equator now. It's nothing tangible, such as seeing the toilets swirl the other way, or recognising a different set of constellations, but is instead a growing feeling that we are more tourists and outsiders than we are wedding guests. We navigate the dirt roads, discussing wedding presents and conferring about Leah's suggestion that we buy the groom's family a medium-sized pig as a goodwill gesture. Instead of selecting china from the registry of Bed, Bath & Beyond, I am in a white van in the Andean mountains cringing as my parents take pictures of women dressed in wool and buy exotic souvenirs that they will take home and hang on the wall. My world has been turned upside down.

We round off the afternoon with a trip to Latacunga's famed market. Every Saturday and Tuesday, people journey from far-off villages to sell cow heads, Nike sweatshirts and old cassette tapes to the Latacungians and those hapless tourists who got on the wrong bus or in a white van and suddenly find themselves in a decidedly not invigorating city in Ecuador.

I join the father and brother of the bride to ostensibly eat but really just stare at *cuy*, an Ecuadorian specialty. *Cuy* is what Americans know as guinea pig; it looks like a rat that has been zapped by a stray electric wire and frozen in time. It is served on its back, four legs raised with paws desperately in need of a manicure. I can't help but think of Leah, who at this minute is getting her nails done in preparation for the wedding, and wonder if she too is a guinea pig in some sort of bizarre cultural experiment.

As the sun sets over Latacunga, we dress for the wedding and I wonder what type of wedding Leah dreamt of when she was a little girl, when she still planned to meet a nice strapping Jewish American boy. Probably long pews packed with visitors, roses and bouquets, a classy band playing 'Hava Nagila', a tow-headed gap-toothed flower girl, and a reception where the bride and groom feed each other cake and smear it on each other's cheeks.

Instead we have a reception room in the hotel/motel, above a room that, judging by the booming bass emanating from below, has already begun to party; an entryway of flowers; 10 Americans dressed in their finest packable wedding wear feeling as nervous as a pack of guinea pigs crossing the Ecuadorian border; and a roomful of Ecuadorians who look like they bite off guinea pigs' heads with their teeth.

After a few brief formalities – limited by the language barriers, and the fact that the parents of the bride and groom don't seem to have much to say to one another – Leah walks down the aisle. I say aisle because the guests are divided as if the line from Mitad del Mundo had been invisibly extended to the parquet dance floor. We Americans stand quietly on one side, the Ecuadorians – and there are dozens of them – just as mute on the other. This set-up has all the characteristics of a battlefield – if someone were to yell charge, I am not at all sure what would happen. We are taller, but there are more of them. And their women wear sharp-looking heels.

The ceremony is over quickly and is mostly in Spanish, leaving the American guests to stare dumbly off into the distance while the Ecuadorian women dab tears from their eyes. The part about there being any reason why these two souls should not be joined in matrimony is definitely done in Spanish, which is wise as most of the American guests are looking surprised that this whole wedding thing is actually happening. There is some Hebrew read, a few Jewish traditions upheld, rings exchanged, and before I know it, the deejay shouts '*Viven los novios!*' and cracks open a bottle of champagne, and the salsa music is pumping.

Before the shock settles in that Leah is now married to an Ecuadorian mechanic who speaks no English, the dance floor erupts into a party of fast-moving couples who know the steps and *man*, can they dance. We Americans shuffle off to the side, shell-shocked, shy. Next to the dark-skinned guests on the other side of the room, we look like white twerps who sit around and watch *Seinfeld* on Saturday nights while the Ecuadorians dance the night away.

But my parents are not ready to give up so quickly. My father, a deejay in his college days, reaches into his jacket pocket and shows me a CD of *Billboard's Top 10 Dance Tunes* he bought at the market earlier that day. He sidles over to the music stand and confers with the deejay by nodding and pointing. He comes back, determined.

'Get ready to dance,' he says to nobody in particular.

We stand watching twirling couples until the pumping beat of Little Eva's 'Locomotion' arouses a cheer from the American side of the room.

Everybody's doing a brand-new dance now...

And the American contingent floods onto the floor, shaking booties and nodding heads with vigour. Finding comfort in solidarity, they form a conga line. The Ecuadorians, more surprised than anything else, step off to the side, not sure what to do. The conga line does a slow but well-meaning lap or two around the dance floor, my father leading, then breaks up so that its members can shake their hips now. I can't help but join them; I feel so embarrassed by my elders trying to have a good time on their own terms that I want to add to their numbers.

Even the Locomotion has to end, but the deejay is skilled, blending the last notes into a techno Latin beat that arouses cheers from the Other Side.

Exit the Americans, enter the Ecuadorians. They pair off and spin and twirl and dip and shake while my parents and the bride's relatives catch their breath. They haven't danced this hard since the sixties, and are sweating and gasping for air in the high mountain altitude.

'Just wait till he plays "Respect",' my dad says, pumping a fist in the air.

The deejay tries a few more Latin melodies before the next *Billboard* song, which is a relief because the bride's dad looks like he might need a bit of a breather and I don't know if they even have an emergency room in Latacunga. But the Americans are back in full force by the first chorus of 'YMCA', which scares the Ecuadorians off to the side again, and shows off the sweat stains in the Americans' armpits. The Ecuadorians don't seem to sweat at all. They are also unsure what's so much fun about spelling Y-M-C-A with your arms.

When it ends, the Americans sit down and the Ecuadorians take over again and I realise I am witnessing two different weddings in two different hemispheres and it's a competition more than it is a celebration of matrimony.

This might have gone on for ever, but we are saved by 'The Electric Slide'. Now it might seem laughable that such a terrible song, and one that stirs up so many memories of middle school and forced line dancing, would serve as the virtual bridge between the north and south. But it doesn't drive the Ecuadorians off the dance floor. And since it is in English, the Americans are obligated to dance too.

Sure, my parents don't remember all of the steps, and the Ecuadorians have a different version that involves a little more hip-shaking and twirling that doesn't work out so well for the bride's uncle, but the reality is that there we are, now relatives by marriage or friendship, boogieing down to the electric slide in a hotel/motel room in Latacunga, Ecuador, while the volcano smokes miles away.

And even this might have been an anomaly had not the groom's cousin, a teenager named Gustavo who had already drunk the equivalent of a bottle of champagne, grabbed my mother before she could even say '*Ole!*' and started tangoing with her on the dance floor. His relatives follow. When the Americans try to institute their exodus at the onset of Latin music, they are waylaid by relatives of the groom who are determined to teach them how to salsa no matter how many times their toes are stomped.

And although I know we'll be leaving tomorrow to go back to Quito and stay in the Hyatt while the Ecuadorians will go back home and thank us for our pig in the morning, I cannot help but appreciate the pull of the equator and its neutralising effect. For as much as we Americans had opposed the wedding, the Ecuadorians probably loathed marrying Jorge off to a family of such terrible dancers as well. And now Leah and Jorge are at latitude zero, able to go any which way, north, south, east or west, and here we are, having crossed the invisible line that first divided us, spinning at

1.667 kilometres per hour near the centre of the world.

I find myself a nice Ecuadorian man whose name I cannot pronounce who is one of the taller men in the room and thus only a head or so shorter than me. He is patient and teaches me how to salsa, and we even add a few bells and whistles of our own after I get the hang of it. I can see my parents raising their eyebrows when he dips me, but I am having too much fun to be embarrassed. We could have danced off until the sunset, or sunrise in this case, had not Leah remembered that she forgot to throw the bouquet, and stopped the dancing so she could line up all the unmarried females to participate.

I stand jockeying with a cluster of Ecuadorian women behind Leah, really more interested in avoiding the flying flowers than catching them. But when she throws them, they hit the ceiling and somehow bounce into my hands.

My Ecuadorian man applauds the loudest and I turn to wink at my parents. Another Ecuadorian wedding. Now wouldn't that be nice.

BAGHDAD TO BASRA, ON THE WRONG SIDE OF THE TRACKS

CÉSAR G SORIANO

Veteran journalist César G Soriano's first trip into Iraq was on a death-defying taxi ride from Kuwait to Baghdad just days after the capital fell to US forces in April 2003. As a former *USA Today* foreign correspondent, he returned to Baghdad regularly to cover the war, surviving one suicide bomb attack in the process. After the security situation improved, César backpacked across Kurdish Iraq to research and write the Iraq chapter of the 2009 Lonely Planet guide to the Middle East. As a freelance journalist, he has also co-authored Lonely Planet guides to Mexico, Colombia, USA and South Korea. The Washington DC native now lives in London with his equally wanderlust wife, Marsha.

I HAVE ALWAYS HAD A LOVE AFFAIR with train travel. There's something romantic about the railways that you just can't experience in a tin can flying 30,000 feet above the ground. I've hopped aboard famous trains – the Marrakesh Express, the London to-Paris Eurostar, the New York subway – and one infamous train: the Iraqi Republic Railway (IRR).

Iraq's national railroad was once the crown jewel of the Middle East's train system. Built in the early 20th century by competing German and British engineers, it provided a vital link between Europe and Asia. Then came two world wars, the Iraq-Iran War and the Gulf War. During the US invasion of Iraq in 2003, rail lines were bombed to bits. What wasn't bombed was stripped by looters. Decades of war and sanctions had finally destroyed the country's fledgling railroad network. But it wasn't long before things looked up again.

Saddam Hussein's regime fell on 9 April, 2003. In the early weeks and months after Saddam, Baghdad was filled with a sense of wonderment as Iraqis discovered what they had been missing. They quickly embraced new technologies like the internet and cell phones, and rediscovered simple pleasures like travelling. For the first time in years, Iraqis had freedom of movement, no longer trapped by invisible ethnic and tribal borders or 'no-fly' zones. Highways reopened. Iraqi Airways returned to the skies. And Iraqi railways were soon rebuilt and back on track.

I was determined to be one of their first paying customers. In the autumn of 2003 I was in Iraq working as a Baghdad correspondent for the newspaper *USA Today,* so first I had to convince my editors that the trip was newsworthy and feasible – and that I wouldn't get blown up in the process. At that time, travelling through Iraq was still relatively safe. The country was not yet mired by insurgency and sectarian warfare; kidnappings and beheadings of Westerners were not yet making headlines. So, on a crisp October morning I headed down to Baghdad Central Station. No bodyguards, no body armor, Kevlar helmet or weapons. Just me, my Iraqi 'fixer' Sabbah and a plastic bag containing our change of clothes and toothbrushes.

Sabbah was a jovial, rotund man in his fifties, a Jack of all trades who worked as a translator, driver and contributing journalist. He knew how to grease the wheels of Iraqi bureaucracy to get things done. And like most Iraqi men of his age, he had served in the Iraq-Iran war of the 1980s. But he was less than enthusiastic about riding the rails. Despite living in Baghdad all his life, he had never once been on a train. Iraqi trains had a reputation of being a poor man's mode of transportation. They were slow, filthy, crowded and unreliable. They were also dirt cheap.

Baghdad Central Station was a dilapidated building with something of a Wild West feel to it. It was a chaotic, dodgy mess of people screaming and shouting, carrying their belongings in plastic bags or ratty old luggage, and pushing and shoving their way through the station. The train waiting on platform two looked like it should have been circling around a Christmas tree. A green-and-yellow, Chinese-made diesel locomotive was hooked up to eight vomit-green passenger cars. All the windows on the train were pockmarked with bullet holes, cracks and, curiously, chewing gum. Several bombed-out train carriages and engines were quietly rusting on the adjacent tracks. One look at the train sent Sabbah into a paroxysm of vocal protests. I was beginning to have second thoughts about my romantic nostalgia for train travel.

The trains from Baghdad went in three directions: north to Mosul through the so-called 'Sunni Triangle of Death', northwest to the Syrian border and south to Basra. We chose Basra as it was the safest and most scenic journey, travelling through the Shiite Muslim holy cities of Karbala and Najaf, then onto the Arab marshlands and Ramallah oil fields and to the port town of Basra. A one-way ticket to Basra was 1000 Iraqi dinars, the equivalent of about 50 US cents. The estimated trip time was 10 hours. The same 300-mile journey by taxi would have taken five hours and cost about US$12, an amount that few Iraqis could afford to pay.

'Absolutely, this train is 100 per cent safe,' the ticket agent assured us. So we boarded it and waited. And waited. The sun grew hotter and the temperature in the non-air-conditioned cars became unbearable. At noon we were ordered to disembark because the train had been cancelled – something about the tracks being sabotaged just south of Baghdad. Or maybe it was a mechanical problem. Different employees gave different answers. 'Maybe tomorrow,' a conductor told us, shrugging his shoulders. 'Yes, come back tomorrow.' Sabbah smiled.

The next morning I dragged Sabbah out of bed and back to the station. Surprisingly, at 8.30am the train departed on time. It was the only thing that would go right all day. The train to Basra was practically empty. Most of the passengers were poor Shiite Muslims, heading south to the Shiite-dominated southern provinces of Iraq. We met some of our fellow passengers. Amad Akal was on his way home to Basra to give his family money that he earned as a janitor at a Baghdad restaurant. Jawad Abbas, a 24-year-old plumber, was going home after a three-day pilgrimage to holy Shiite shrines in Najaf, Karbala and Baghdad.

'It's completely inhumane to make us spend all this time on the train without air-conditioning or basic services,' Abbas said. By ignoring the country's railroads and focussing its energy and resources on the aviation industry, Iraqi's Ministry of Tourism was taking from the poor and giving to the rich, he said.

It took us nearly an hour just to get out of Baghdad, a sprawling city of nearly seven million people. Beyond its shantytowns and squalor, we finally reached the countryside, passing village after village of mud huts and long fields of palm trees. About an hour south of Baghdad, the train approached a few dozen people walking alongside the tracks carrying banners. The few dozen became a few hundred, then several thousand. The train slowed to a crawl as we lumbered past a sea of humanity. They were Shiite pilgrims, all heading to Karbala, and all on foot. They were the poorest of the poor, unable to afford even the 50¢ train fare. Most were clad all in black, some wore sandals but many were barefoot. Some carried green flags and black banners with Arabic script of Quran verses or names of dead relatives. They clapped and chanted and seemed happier than those of us stuck on the slow-moving train.

Every now and then, a pilgrim would hop aboard. The conductor and two Iraqi policemen patrolling the train seemed oblivious to the fare-jumpers. 'We never throw anybody off,' Wathek Sattar said as he made his rounds to collect tickets. 'If it looks like they can pay, we will make them pay double. If they are poor, we let them stay.'

Travelling on Iraqi Railways was not exactly the Orient Express. The old train had few amenities. There were no lights. Most of the seats were missing armrests. The toilets were simple holes in the floor that dumped directly onto the tracks below. There were no platforms between cars, so passengers had to carefully hop across an empty void, risking ending up on the tracks. There were no couchettes, no cafe and definitely no bar. I had only brought a small bottle of water and no food with me. Clearly, I had not planned well. Luckily, one of the train attendants was making a few dinars on the side by selling tea to passengers. He carried a teapot and a bucket of filthy water, which he used to wash the three teacups that were shared by all the passengers. He heated his teapot on a rusting kerosene stove and tank, dangerously perched in the aisle of a crowded passenger car. By noon my stomach was growling and I had become increasingly cranky. An old man across from me happily offered half his sandwich, but I felt guilty about accepting food from someone with so little.

When we reached the station in Karbala, a gaggle of young men hopped on board to sell sandwiches, water and cigarettes to thirsty and hot passengers. After a few minutes, the conductor blew his whistle, a signal for the vendors to jump off the train before it began moving out. But a few of the salesmen stayed on for the long haul. One of them was Akmed Shati. He claimed to be 13 years old, but looked much younger. Every Friday on his day off from school, he told me, he rode the train alone from Basra to Karbala and back home to Basra to earn money for his family. He carried a small plastic cooler from which he sold water, Italian ice, beer, juice and soda. On this day, the little entrepreneur said he had made 35,000 dinars (about US$18) – a fortune by Iraqi standards.

There was not much to do but stare out the window at one dusty village after another, so Sabbah and I spent most of our time talking to other passengers. 'The Sheik' would not give me his real name but spent an hour ranting on about the evils of the United States – in fluent Spanish. He said he had spent several years working in Latin America for a nongovernmental organisation. Then there was Natak Jabar and his cousin Younis Sabah, both 21, both dressed in traditional long white robes, *dishdashas*. We found them sitting in one of the long freight cars, the cargo doors open and their legs dangling over the sides. Next to them was a large pile of what looked like fishing nets. Sure enough, Sabah, Jabar, and Jabar's five brothers were all fishermen, on their way to the Persian Gulf. Their plan, Jabar said, was to spend three days fishing, then return to their home in Suq Ash Shuyukh to sell their catch.

Jabar, Sabah and most of the male passengers passed the time on the long train ride by chain-smoking. It wasn't long before the carriages were thick with smoke. For nonsmokers like me, relief could only be found by sticking our heads out of the cracked windows or putting our noses to one of the many bullet holes. Despite all this, across the aisle from me, Abdul Yaseen, his wife and their four children were ecstatic about their first-ever train adventure. They were returning home to Basra after attending a wedding near Baghdad. 'I like the train because it's more comfortable, slow and lets the kids have a chance to see the countryside,' he said. His wide-eyed children were peering from the windows, wearing their best clothes, reminiscent of a time when travelling was actually an occasion for dressing up. Abdul's nine-year-old daughter, Haba, surprised to see an American on board, latched onto us and peppered me with questions in broken English: 'Mister, where you from? You married? You have children? You like Arabian music? You like Jennifer Lopez? Mister, buy me Pepsi!'

Around 4pm the train pulled into the station in Nasiriyah,

one of the largest cities in southern Iraq. But, unlike our stops at other cities, the train did not immediately pull out but sat at the platform. And sat. And sat. There was no announcement or explanation for our delay. The thermometer on the platform read 100°F. Inside, the train was becoming a steel oven, baking us alive. Within minutes, we were drenched in sweat. The stench of body odor, dirty baby diapers and the raw sewage on the tracks became unbearable. An old woman fainted and was carried outside into the shade and doused with water, and many more of us followed her out into the air. Angry passengers took out their rage on the conductor, who explained that the station manager had refused to give clearance for the train to proceed. Apparently there was only one working track between Nasiriyah and Basra, and a northbound cargo train already had dibs. An hour later, without a whistle or warning, the train began pulling out of the station. Of course, most of us were still out on the platform and had to run and jump back onto the moving train.

South of Nasiriyah, we reached the most scenic point of the journey. The endless monochrome images of brown, dusty villages were replaced by lush, green landscape, fields of corn, alfalfa and date palms. This was the Arab Marshland, a fertile region between the Tigris and Euphrates Rivers that is the legendary location of the Garden of Eden. The setting sun blazed into the windows of the right side of the train. There were no curtains or shades to pull down, so passengers took chewing gum from their mouths and used it to stick newspapers onto the windows to shield their heads from the sun. Ah, so that was why there was gum stuck all over the windows.

At dusk, the train pulled into Suq Ash Shuyukh, a town known for its conservative population who were less than thrilled with the American occupation of Iraq. Dozens of young men were loitering on both sides of the tracks. Peering out the window, I noticed several of them were making threatening gestures, as if pointing rifles at us. It was a tense situation and the train did not stop long. The moment we pulled out of the station, there was a loud crash from the next passenger car. Somebody had thrown a brick through the window, raining glass on a 15-year-old bride and her 25-year-old groom. The bride, Akbal Hussein, received a small cut on her left cheek. Iraqi policemen rushed to her assistance and searched for the culprit, but by then the assailant had melted into the crowd. The conductor, Ziyad Khalaf, sheepishly admitted that this was the third attack on the train in as many days, despite the assurances I had received from staff in Baghdad. 'My supervisors never worry about passengers. They only worry about their desks in their air-conditioned office,' he said, expressing rare public contempt for his superiors.

For IRR employees, the US invasion of Iraq was fairly lucrative. Khalaf proudly boasted that he was now making $60 a month, a big increase on the $8 a month he earned under Saddam Hussein's regime. But, despite US President George W Bush's pledge of millions to improve Iraq's railroad system, which his administration described as presenting 'a seriously negative public image', precious little money was being spent to improve and upgrade it. 'There was a time when everything was completely new and the trains were full of passengers. But when Iraq started its wars with its neighbours, everything began to decline,' said Khalaf, who began working with IRR in 1977.

We made our way to the locomotive to meet Hamad Khader, sitting in the driver's seat of this green machine. This 30-year-old recalled boyhood memories of playing with toy trains and his dreams of becoming a locomotive engineer. He began working for IRR as a ticket taker and conductor, working his way up to engineer. 'It used to be such an exciting job,' Khader said. 'But now, I have no interest. It's risky. It's dangerous. It's just a job.'

The interior of the train turned pitch black when the sun went down. The only source of illumination was the occasional flicker of a lighter or burning cigarette. Quietness descended as passengers settled into sleep. But no sooner had I drifted into dreamland than we were awaked by a howling noise: a dust storm. A giant brown cloud enveloped the train and threatened to shake it off its tracks. Every door and window of the train was open, and it didn't take long for the passenger cars to fill with dust. I coughed and hacked my lungs out for the remainder of the trip.

Near the end of our journey, the darkness was replaced by an orange and blue glow as the train passed through the Ramallah oil fields. The desert seemed to be on fire as we looked at the amazing sight of hundreds of pilot flames burning atop oil wells. This was the heart of Iraq's economy, the source of all of its riches – and of all of its miseries.

Just before 8pm the train chugged into Basra Central Station, nearly 12 hours after our departure. 'This is the absolute last time I will ever take the train,' complained Abdul Yaseen, who earlier had shared with us his love of this form of travel. Tired, hungry and filthy, Sabbah and I stumbled off the train and walked to a nearby hotel for the night. The next morning we returned to Baghdad, this time by taxi.

Iraq's post-war railroad never really caught on with passengers. The trains routinely left stations empty and were regularly attacked by insurgents. In 2004 and 2005 rebels began a campaign of blowing up train tracks in an effort to stop the transport of military equipment. Finally, in the spring of 2006, passenger trains were discontinued altogether. But despite the lack of business, the IRR continued to look to the future. It spent millions of US tax dollars to refurbish Baghdad Central Station and replace train equipment. In December 2007, with security dramatically improving, passenger trains quietly returned to service. As of 2008 passengers had slowly begun returning to the rails. But most are still scared away by violence and, now, high ticket prices. The fare from Baghdad to Basra has skyrocketed from 50¢ to $3.50. That's inflation for you. But it still works out to about 1¢ a mile, making it one of the cheapest train services in the world.

Would I take the Iraq train again? Ask me in another 10 years.

A VISIT TO KANASANKATAN

JASON ELLIOT

Jason Elliot's first book, *An Unexpected Light: Travels in Afghanistan*, won the Thomas Cook/*Daily Telegraph* Travel Book award and was a *New York Times* bestseller. His latest book is *Mirrors of the Unseen: Journeys in Iran*. He lives in London.

AT THE END OF A LONG JOURNEY in the Middle East, I received a message from an English friend I hadn't seen for years. Would I like to visit him on my way back home? He was now living, as he put it, at the point where the Arab and African worlds meet, and promised it would be worth the detour. 'Come to Kanasankatan,' he said. 'It's not at all what you would expect.'

A follow-up phone call piqued my curiosity. The capital was said to have originated as a remote outpost of the Roman Empire, and its terrible climate had made it the least favourite of its imperial occupiers. Centuries ago, its seafaring natives had achieved notoriety for their pugnacity, greed and nautical prowess. By the sound of it, things hadn't changed all that much: in the area where my friend lived, the only form of law had, until very recently, been enforced by rival gangs. Even the police hadn't dared to appear there until a few years ago; this was said to be a particular source of local pride.

I agreed to visit, knowing it would be my last glimpse of the East for a good while. Diverting my journey home, I called on arrival at the airport. A combination of train and bus would bring me to the right part of the city, explained my friend. But his directions were disconcertingly vague. 'Just ask for the "Tower of Terror",' he quipped, explaining that, at 30 storeys, the apartment block where he lived was nothing short of a national landmark. 'Used to be the most popular place for suicides. Murders too. Try to get here before dark, and use your Arabic if you need to.'

It was the end of summer; people looked weary and sapped by the heat. In the late afternoon, a Somali bus driver with a terrifying disregard for pedestrian life dropped me at a crossroads in the capital. A trio of veiled women, each cradling a sleeping infant, descended with me, speaking a language I had never before heard. I followed a street named after a thousand-year-old saint, and asked directions from passersby. Two men spoke no English; a third was a deaf-mute, and didn't speak at all. On a cobbled side-street lined with stunted acacia, the air shook with the noise of a pneumatic drill. A truck was being loaded with bits of road, and a hopelessly inefficient team of workmen were excavating broken pipes in water-filled craters. I felt a pang of pity for the residents, and marvelled at the natives' indifference to dust and noise.

Further on, I could hear the cackle of seagulls from overhead. There was the smell of rotting fish, and a street sign which, translated, read 'Port of Beauty'. To the north, a long, straight road ran towards railway tracks and a filthy canal. Century-old brick buildings rose on either side, their neglected window-frames and lintels all slightly askew. The shops beneath them bore signs in quaintly misspelled English, or in Arabic letters that I could just decipher as I walked along: Thobani Chemist, Halal butcher, Ka-na-san-ka-tan Mosque. All the smells of the East seemed to be represented there: turmeric-laden vapours from ill-lit kitchens, the oily smoke of grilling kebabs, the occasional whiff of marijuana and, from a tiny stall where a turbaned man was selling Qurans, rose-scented incense. The entire street was lined with stalls selling secondhand clothes and used furniture, broken radios, 50-pound sacks of rice, and pyramids of fruits and vegetables that I couldn't identify.

I wondered what I might learn about a nation from a single street? It was always hard to know. I felt the gaze of watchful men who looked as though they spent the entire day puffing silently at their water-pipes. I wondered if I could detect hostility in their eyes; perhaps it was no more than weary indifference at the sight of an outsider. I felt pale and conspicuous. Arabic, several African languages, and Portuguese were being spoken all around me. There were dark-skinned men in striped cloaks and slippers, and women in gowns and veils of various kinds. One woman's veil – an ancestral memory, perhaps, of the days when the Arabs had fought their way across the untamed portions of Africa – was hemmed in imitation leopard-skin. Another, but for the dark eyes behind an opening like an arrow-slit, concealed all. Crouched in anonymous doorways, beggars and the dispossessed muttered pleas for loose change.

For a private challenge, I decided to buy a joint of meat and present it to my friend. The butcher was a big, bearded man with a crater-like scar in the centre of his forehead. I explained I wanted lamb. He disappeared and returned with a split-open carcass over his shoulder, sharpening his knife as I pointed to the leg.

He asked what country I was from, and whether I were a Muslim. 'You would make a good Muslim,' he chuckled, as he cut into the meat.

What was life like here? I asked. He shook his head gently and, between sighs, recounted the ills of the nation. Its leader was deeply unpopular but refused to relinquish power; worse, there was no one fit to replace him. His compatriots were dying in an unpopular war financed by international criminals; the economy was out of control; and not long ago, suicide bombs had killed a score of people in the capital.

Handing over a fraction of what I would have paid in central London, I thanked him and left, suddenly remembering the colloquial expression of appreciation.

'Che zmayt!'

'Che zmayt!' he beamed back.

Further along, a couple of teenage boys were standing beside the entrance to a mosque.

'As-salaamu aleikum.'

'Wa aleikum salaam.'

Wanting directions, I asked the elder boy if he spoke Arabic.

'Akurs afakindo.' This was an affirmation, in the local dialect. I asked if he knew the whereabouts of the 'Tower of Terror'.

'Yakan faki n'missit kanya,' he said, waving an arm in the direction of the ancient iron railway bridge. He was right: beyond the tracks, unmistakably, rose the tower. It was a brutal-looking rectangle of brown concrete, peaked with a sheaf of bristling antennae. In scale it had the starkness of a Cold War military headquarters. A desultory geometry of washing lines, strung up and down its balconies, gave it a look of moth-eaten patchwork. It was a relic of the years when Soviet influence had been at its height in the region; yet the locals were said to be as proud of it as Parisians of the Eiffel Tower.

It was a grim-looking setting. To the east stretched long identical rows of government housing, wedged at their far end under a section of elevated highway. There was a squeal and rattle of train as I crossed the bridge and, just there, amid the graffiti and peeling posters, the wind-blown refuse and architecture devoid of even the memory of beauty, I felt a stab of resentment for the people who had allowed their culture to be claimed by the anonymity of such ugliness. It was a depressing revelation – that four-and-a-half billion years of terrestrial evolution had come to this. But it was a scene replicated in cities all over the world; I had seen so many others like it, where the sum of human endeavour seems so hideously overrated, and where life seems likely to survive any catastrophe virtually unchanged, as cockroaches have been predicted to do. Proof, in short – if it were one day confirmed that there was indeed a divine scheme behind the existence of humanity – that the scheme had gone definitively awry. I had been to this place in a thousand other places; I was in all of them now, and they were no different. I was nowhere.

The tower loomed up; I reached the entrance and, over a faulty intercom, began a frustrating negotiation with the African guard who spoke only a few words of English. Eventually I heard my friend's voice, was buzzed inside, and headed towards the 20th floor in the single functioning lift. I found his apartment at the end of a long corridor, passing, at every doorway, the unidentifiable fragrance of an evening meal in preparation.

My friend greeted me with a smile and a glass of chilled Sancerre. I felt deeply relieved. 'Welcome to the Tower,' he said. 'Let's go onto the balcony. It'll help you to get your bearings.'

Far below, I could make out the mosque I had earlier caught sight of, where the evening light now struck a band of tiled calligraphy on its roof, and an ant-like procession of men were filing towards the entrance. I felt a long way from home. We gazed over the panorama beyond, and my friend pointed out the city's monuments.

'Look,' he said, pointing to a slender spike on the horizon.

'You can just see Big Ben.'

It was true. His outstretched hand led my eye in a sweeping arc above the river Thames, resting for a few moments in turn on Westminster Abbey, the pyramidal glow of Vauxhall Cross, and the pale and hollow towers of Battersea power station.

'People don't believe me when I tell them this is Kensington,' he said gloomily.

'But this is W.10,' I said. 'Strictly speaking, it's North Kensington.'

He waved away this distinction with a look of disdain, and refilled my glass.

'Next time, don't come via Portobello Road,' he advised me. 'Get the bus from Victoria Station. It stops outside the door, just where it says "Trellick Tower".'

My friend was quite right: it was not what I had expected. For a few minutes we watched the planes sinking towards eye level on their final approach towards Heathrow airport, and then, as it grew cooler, moved back indoors.

LOOKING FOR ABDELATI
TANYA SHAFFER

Tanya Shaffer's book *Somebody's Heart is Burning: A Woman Wanderer in Africa,* was called 'the best…of recent adventure books penned by women' by *Vogue* magazine and chosen by the *San Francisco Chronicle* as one of the Best Books of 2003. Her stories have appeared on Salon.com and in numerous anthologies, including *Travelers' Tales Books' Best Travel Writing 2007* and *Best Women's Travel Writing 2007.* An award-winning playwright and solo performer, Tanya has toured internationally with her solo shows *Let My Enemy Live Long!* and *Miss America's Daughters* and her play *Brigadista.* Her play *Baby Taj* is available in print from Samuel French, Inc. Visit her online queendom at www.TanyaShaffer.com.

'Looking for Abdelati' © by Tanya Shaffer. First published on Salon .com and subsequently published in the memoir *Somebody's Heart Is Burning* Vintage Books, 2003.

HERE'S WHAT I LOVE ABOUT TRAVEL: strangers get a chance to amaze you. Sometimes a single day can bring a blooming surprise, a simple kindness that opens a chink in the brittle shell of your heart and makes you a different person when you go to sleep – more tender, less jaded – than the one you were when you woke up.

This particular day began when Miguel and I descended from a cramped, cold bus at 7am and walked the stinking grey streets of Casablanca with our backpacks, looking for food. Six days earlier I had finished a stint on a volunteer project, creating a public park in Kenitra, an ugly industrial city on the Moroccan coast. This was my final day of travel before hopping on a plane to sub-Saharan Africa and more volunteer work.

Miguel was one of five non-Moroccans on the work project, a 21-year-old vision of flowing brown curls and buffed golden physique. Although having him as a travelling companion took care of any problems I might have encountered with Moroccan men, he was inordinately devoted to his girlfriend, Eva, a wonderfully brassy, wiry, chain-smoking Older Woman of 25 with a husky Scotch-drinker's voice, whom he couldn't go more than half an hour without mentioning. Unfortunately, Eva had had to head back to Barcelona immediately after the three-week work camp ended, and Miguel wanted to explore Morocco. Since I was the only other person on the project who spoke Spanish, and he spoke no French or Arabic, his tight orbit shifted onto me, and we became travelling companions. This involved posing as a married couple at hotels, which made Miguel so uncomfortable that the frequency of his references to Eva went from half-hour to 15-minute intervals, and then five as we got closer to bedtime. Finally one night, as we set up in our room in Fès, I took him by the shoulders and said, 'Miguel, it's okay. You're a handsome man, but I'm over 21. I can handle myself, I swear.'

This morning we were going to visit Abdelati, a sweet, gentle young man we'd worked with on the project in Kenitra. He'd been expecting us to arrive in Casablanca for a few days, and since he had no telephone, he'd written down his address and told us to just show up – his mother and sisters were always at home. Since my plane was leaving from Casablanca the following morning, we wanted to get an early start so we could spend the whole day with him.

Unlike the romantic image its name conjured, Casablanca was a thoroughly modern city, with rectangular high-rises sprouting everywhere and wide boulevards already jammed with cars. Horns blared, and the air was thick with heat and exhaust. My T-shirt, pinned to my skin by my backpack, was soaked with sweat. Eventually we scored some croissants and overly sugared *panaches* (a mix of banana, apple and orange juice) at a roadside cafe, where the friendly proprietor advised us to take a taxi rather than a bus out to Abdelati's neighbourhood. He said the taxi should cost about 20 dirham – under three dollars – and the buses would take all day.

It took us an hour to find a cab. When we did, the poker-faced driver informed us that the address which Abdelati had written down for us was somehow suspect. When we got to the neighbourhood, he told us, we would have to ask directions.

'Here we go,' Miguel whispered, rolling his eyes. 'Eva would hate this.'

First the driver asked a cop, who scratched his head and asked our nationalities, looking at our grimy faces and scraggly attire with bemused tolerance. After more small talk, he pointed vaguely to a park a few blocks away. There a group of barefoot seven- or eight-year-old boys were kicking a soccer ball. Our driver asked where Abdelati's house was and one of the boys said Abdelati had moved, but he could take us to the new house.

This seemed a bit odd to me, since Abdelati had just given me the address a week ago, but since a similar thing had happened in Fès, I chalked it up as another Moroccan mystery and didn't worry about it too much.

The little boy came with us in the cab, full of his own importance, squirming and twisting to wave at other children as we inched down the narrow, winding roads. Finally the little boy pointed to a house, and our driver went to the door and inquired. He came back to the cab saying Abdelati's sister was in this house visiting friends and would come along to show us where they lived.

Soon a lovely, delicate-featured girl of about 16 emerged from the house. She was dressed in a Western skirt and blouse, which surprised me since Abdelati's strong religious beliefs and upright demeanour had made me think he came from a more traditional family. Another thing that surprised me was her skin colour. Whereas Abdelati looked very African, this young woman was an olive-skinned Arab. Still, I'd seen other unusual familial combinations in Morocco's complex racial mosaic, so I didn't give it too much thought.

We soon arrived at another house where Abdelati's sister directed our taxi driver to stop. We waited in the front yard while the sister went in and returned accompanied by her mother, sisters and brother-in-law, all of whom greeted us with cautious warmth. Unlike the younger girl, the older sisters wore traditional robes, though their faces were not veiled. You see a range of orthodoxy in Moroccan cities, caught as they are between Europe and the Arab world. From the younger sister's skirt and blouse to the completely veiled women gliding through the streets with only their eyes in view, the women's outfits embody the entire spectrum.

We paid our taxi driver, and I tipped and thanked him profusely, until he grew embarrassed and drove away.

We were ushered into a pristine middle-class Moroccan home, with an intricately carved doorway and swirling multicoloured tiles lining the walls. The mother told us in broken French that Abdelati was out, but would be home soon. We sat on low, cushioned seats in the living room, drinking sweet, pungent mint tea poured at a suitable height from a tiny silver teapot and eating sugar cookies, while the family members took turns sitting with us and making shy, polite conversation that frequently lapsed into uncomfortable silence. Every time anything was said, Miguel would say '*Qué pasó?*' with extreme eagerness, and I would translate the mundane fragment into Spanish for him: 'Nice weather today. Tomorrow perhaps rain.' At this he'd sink back into fidgety frustration, undoubtedly wishing Eva were there.

An hour passed, and as the guard kept changing, more family members emerged from inner rooms. I was again struck by the fact that they were all light-skinned Arabs. How did Abdelati fit into this picture? Was he adopted? I was very curious to find out.

After two hours had passed with no sign of Abdelati, the family insisted on serving us a meal of couscous and fish. The food was a delectable blend of sweet and savoury, with plump raisins, cayenne pepper, slivered almonds and loads of garlic.

'Soon,' was the only response I got when I inquired as to what time he might arrive.

'You come to the *hammam*, the bath,' the younger sister said after we'd finished lunch. 'When we finish, he is back.'

'The bath?' I asked, looking around the apartment.

The sister laughed. 'The women's bath!' she said. 'Haven't you been yet?'

She pointed at Miguel. 'He can go to the men's; it's right next door.'

'*Qué pasó?*' said Miguel anxiously, sitting up.

'She wants to take us to the baths,' I said.

A look of abject horror crossed his face. 'The-the bath?' he stammered. 'You and me?'

'Yes,' I said, smiling widely. 'Is there some problem?'

'Well...well...'

I watched his agitation build for a moment, then sighed and put my hand over his. 'Separate baths, Miguel. You with the men, me with the women.'

'Oh.' He almost giggled with relief. 'Of course.'

The women's bath consisted of three large connecting rooms, each one hotter and steamier than the last, until you could barely see a metre in front of you. The floors were filled with naked women of all ages and body types, sitting directly on the slippery

84

tiles, washing each other with mitts made of rough washcloths. Tiny girls and babies sat in plastic buckets filled with soapy water – their own pint-sized tubs. The women carried empty buckets, swinging like elephants' trunks, to and from the innermost room where they filled them at a stone basin from a spigot of boiling water, mixing in a little cold from a neighbouring spigot to temper it.

In a culture where the body is usually covered, I was surprised by the women's absolute lack of inhibition. They sat, mostly in pairs, pouring the water over their heads with small plastic pitchers, then scrubbing each other's backs – and I mean scrubbing. Over and over they attacked the same spot, as though they were trying to get out a particularly stubborn stain, leaving reddened flesh in their wake. They sprawled across each other's laps. They washed each other's fronts, backs, arms, legs. Some women washed themselves as though they were masturbating, hypnotically circling the same spot. Two tiny girls, who were about four years old, scrubbed their grandmother who lay sprawled across the floor face down. A prepubescent girl lay in her mother's lap, belly up, eyes closed, as relaxed as a cat, while her mother applied a forceful up and down stroke across the entire length of her daughter's torso. I was struck by one young woman in particular who reclined alone like a beauty queen in a tanning salon, back arched, head thrown back, right at the steamy heart of the baths, where the air was almost suffocating. She soaped her breasts in sensual circles, proudly, her stomach held in, long chestnut hair rippling down her back, a goddess in her domain.

Abdelati's sister, whose name was Samara, went at my back with her mitt, which felt like steel wool.

'Ow!' I cried out. 'Careful!'

This sent her into gales of laughter that drew the attention of the surrounding women, who saw what was happening and joined her in appreciative giggles as she continued to sandblast my skin.

'You must wash more often,' she said, pointing to the refuse of her work – little grey scrolls of dead skin that clung to my arms like lint on a sweater.

When it came time to switch roles, I tried to return the favour, but after a few moments Samara became impatient with my wimpiness and grabbed the washcloth herself, still laughing. After washing the front of her body she called over a friend to wash her back while she giggled and sang.

'What was it like in there?' asked Miguel when we met again outside. After his visit to the men's baths he looked pink and damp as a newborn, and I wondered whether his experience was anything like mine.

'I'd like to tell you all about it,' I said eagerly, 'but...' I paused for emphasis, then leaned in and whispered, 'I don't think Eva would approve.'

When we got back to the house, the mother, older sister and uncle greeted us at the door.

'Please,' said the mother, 'Abdelati is here.'

'Oh, good,' I said, and for a moment, before I walked into the living room, his face danced in my mind – the warm brown eyes, the smile so shy and gentle and filled with radiant life.

We entered the lovely tiled room we'd sat in before, and a handsome young Arab man in nicely pressed Western pants and shirt came forward to shake our hands with an uncertain expression on his face.

'*Bonjour, mes amis,*' he said cautiously.

'*Bonjour,*' I smiled, slightly confused. '*Abdelati – est-ce qu'il est ici?*' Is Abdelati here?

'*Je suis Abdelati.*'

'But...but...' I looked from him to the family and then began to giggle tremulously. 'I...I'm sorry. I'm afraid we've made a bit of a mistake. I...I'm so embarrassed.'

'*Qué? Qué pasó?*' Miguel asked urgently. 'I don't understand. Where is he?'

'We got the wrong Abdelati,' I told him, then looked around at the assembled family who'd spent the better part of a day entertaining us. 'I'm afraid we don't actually know your son.'

For a split second no one said anything, and I wondered

whether I might implode right then and there and blow away like a pile of ash.

Then the uncle exclaimed heartily, '*Ce n'est pas grave!*'

'Yes,' the mother joined in. 'It doesn't matter at all. Won't you stay for dinner, please?'

I was so overwhelmed by their kindness that tears rushed to my eyes. For all they knew we were con artists, thieves, anything. Would such a thing ever happen in the US?

Still, with my plane leaving the next morning, I felt the moments I could share with the first Abdelati and his family slipping further and further away.

'Thank you so much,' I said fervently. 'It's been a beautiful, beautiful day, but please... Could you help me find this address?'

I took out the piece of paper Abdelati had given me back in Kenitra, and the new Abdelati, his uncle and his brother-in-law came forward to decipher it.

'This is Baalal Abdelati!' said the second Abdelati with surprise. 'We went to school together! He lives less than a kilometre from here. I will bring you to his house.'

And that is how it happened, that after taking photos and exchanging addresses and hugs and promises to write, Miguel and I left our new-found family and arrived at the home of our friend Abdelati as the last orange streak of sunset was fading into the indigo night. There I threw myself into the arms of that dear and lovely young man, exclaiming, 'I thought we'd never find you!'

After greetings had been offered all around, and the two Abdelatis had shared stories and laughter, we waved goodbye to our new friend Abdelati and entered a low, narrow hallway, lit by kerosene lamps.

'This is my mother,' said Abdelati.

And suddenly I found myself caught up in a crush of fabric and spice, gripped in the tight embrace of a completely veiled woman, who held me and cried over me and wouldn't let me go, just as though I were her own daughter, and not a stranger she'd never before laid eyes on in her life.

WANGARA'S CROSS

JOSHUA CLARK

Joshua Clark is the author of *Heart Like Water: Surviving Katrina and Life in its Disaster Zone*, a finalist for the National Book Critics Circle award. He covered New Orleans in Hurricane Katrina's aftermath for Salon.com and National Public Radio. Clark, the founder of Light of New Orleans Publishing, has edited such books as *French Quarter Fiction*, *Southern Fried Divorce*, and others, including most recently *Louisiana: In Words*. He has contributed to many publications and anthologies including *The Best American Nonrequired Reading*, *Poets & Writers*, the *Los Angeles Times*, *Boston Globe*, *Chicago Tribune*, *Philadelphia Inquirer*, *Miami Herald*, and he represented Louisiana in *State by State: A Panoramic Portrait of America*.

THERE IS A PART of the Simpson Desert in Central Australia where day is split clean into red and blue, earth and sky, with only bone-white trees between the two. And dusk is the same as dawn. The small leafless trees reach like hands, the branches fingers grasping for sky, silhouetted against the red above the horizon. Above the red is a strip of orange and above that canary yellow and pastel blue which gets deeper, then darker overhead, until it's black against clouds of stars you can't see in the Northern Hemisphere. It was below those stars and between those trees that my overturned '74 panel van lay hulking against the red horizon.

I hadn't been near it since noon, when the world was still split clean between red and blue, when the van had stopped being an extension of my body, as cars usually are, and started being a three-tonne hunk of metal that you're trapped inside while it's succumbing to the forces of gravity after you've helicoptered off the road and walloped your third tree.

I hadn't even been going fast. Over the last eight days I'd lost traction and spun out four times on the dirt roads here. But there was nothing to hit, just dirt and sky to slide through until I stopped. And trees. It was the trees that got me. That third one anyway.

When the van started rolling, I thought that was it. But I also thought about how, if I lived, this would make a good story I could tell my girlfriend sometime. Like most people, I'd often wondered what I'd think about right before I died. And that was it. A story.

When the van finished rolling I realised there was blood all over my shoulder and I was probably in shock. I did a limb check. Then a broken bone check. Then I tried to open the door but it wouldn't budge. There was ground where the window used to be. I turned the other way to see sky where the passenger-side window used to be. Both doors, along with the sides of the van, were caved in. After making my way through my belongings heaped on top of me – bottles of water, a gas can, canned beans, CD cases, books, clothes, pillows, a cooler –

I kicked open the passenger door, climbed up, leaped from the van and started running like hell because as everyone knows from the movies your car always blows up after you have a bad accident.

It didn't blow up. It just lay there on its side exhaling Cyndi Lauper. It was part of a CD mix my girlfriend had given me for the trip. My finger had been on the way to hitting the 'skip' button when the van lost traction. I'd always wondered if the stereo would keep going after you got into an accident.

Finally, the song ended. For five seconds there was silence in the thin, still July winter sun. I inspected my shoulder, and saw it was only a scrape. Then the synthesiser and drum machine started up again and Cyndi kicked into gear. Something somehow in the tumult must have hit the 'repeat' button.

When I lifted my head from my hands I found myself staring at a pair of emus, each a good six feet tall. They regarded me with curiosity, their fist-sized heads bobbing up and down on spaghetti necks. They were likely not used to seeing college kids covered in red dirt, bleeding and crying about the prospect of having to listen to Cyndi Lauper for infinity. And I was naked. I hadn't seen a person in two days and it felt pretty cool to be driving around naked. Not that it made a difference to the emus. They sniffed through the debris left in the van's wake from the road – my camera in pieces, more CD cases, more canned beans, more books, bottles of water, a compass, underwear, a boot, two pairs of shattered sunglasses, pens, paper, a cowboy hat, coins, cash, until they reached the van itself and got an earful of Cyndi's chorus. At that, the emus ran off to wherever it is they run off to. Me, I had nowhere to go. The next town was about 200 kilometres away. I picked up a pair of underpants that had fallen out of the van and put them on. The cowboy hat and the one (right) boot too. And waited.

Now, while patches of the Milky Way blossomed overhead, and the red of the desert was hugging the bottom of the sky, Cyndi was informing me of exactly how much fun girls just wanna have for the seventy-fourth time. It was getting cold. The matches were still somewhere in the van, next to my mattress, along with all my other worldly belongings. The thing had eaten them all. It had tried to eat me. And I felt like it might get up at any time and have another go at it. But I needed those matches for a fire. Then I saw the smallest blob of light on the horizon, as if the sun was coming back for me at the end of the road. Headlights.

It took a long time before the lights got any bigger, and then impossibly long before I could see the camper van. The red sank below the horizon, then the orange, and finally the canary yellow. The sky was all black and blue and stars by the time the camper van got me in its headlights.

I flailed my arms wildly as though they might not notice some bleeding guy standing in the middle of the road in the middle of nowhere in his underwear, one boot and a cowboy hat. They came within three metres of me and stopped. Blinded in the headlights, I heard the windows roll up. Then the doors lock. Did this look like a carjacking to them? I pointed to my van. The camper van, the size of a small home, crept towards me nervously over the lumpy dirt and rocks that made up the road. It pulled up alongside me. The window came down and from within the dark interior a small voice asked, 'What in God's name is that noise?'

'That's Cyndi Lauper, sir,' I said.

'Sounds like Satan,' he said.

'You're telling me, sir.'

'What's a Canadian doing out here?'

'American, sir.'

'America?!' said another voice, a woman, from a bit further back in the darkness, probably the passenger seat. 'Graceland?'

'Nope. New Haven, Connecticut, ma'am.'

'Oh.'

'Connecticut?' said the man. 'No kidding? We've been to Detroit before. Went to a dry-cleaning convention there in '84.'

'Really.'

'Do they still have Old Landmark Church of God in Christ there?'

'Not really sure.'

'Have you been to Graceland?' asked the woman. 'We've been to Graceland.'

'Nope,' I said. 'Anyway, I'm kinda bleeding and cold and my van's over there on its side and –'

'What are you doing in Australia?' asked the man. I could make out the top of his bald head now, and the woman's silhouette – big glasses and big hair.

'I was spending a semester abroad,' I said. 'Studying at the Queensland College of Art. Just got done and wanted to see the country before I have to go back to the States and my van's over there on its – '

'Just travelling ourselves. Bought this campervan after we retired four years ago, started driving and forgot to stop. This is our fifth lap round the bush. We keep it at a slow clip, that way it stays right-side up. I'm Joseph and this is Mary.'

'Josh.'

'Well, Josh, where in God's name are your clothes?'

'In the van.'

Silence. I didn't feel like explaining that I had become scared to death of my own car. Then he said, 'Well, Josh, did you see that sign way back there at the start of the desert that said "Four-wheel drive vehicles only, contact police before you begin and when you get through" or something like that?'

'Yup.'

'Was your van four-wheel drive?'

'Nope.'

'Did you contact the police?'

'Nope.'

'Connecticut, huh?'

'Yup.'

Joseph opened the door, smiling. He was a cherubic old man

with a thin horseshoe of white hair around his head. He got an enormous chain out of the back and we fixed it to the trailer behind their camper van. First we turned my van right-side up, put two of their spare tyres on it, then dragged it to the road. I picked up my belongings from the ground, tossed them into the van, and we set off towards what they said was a small town ahead. The beast seemed a lot less menacing now that it was on a leash. It resembled a gargantuan, crinkled egg blasting Cyndi Lauper as we putted along in second gear.

To this day I can't recall much that was said in that campervan. But I remember they were good people. I remember they said they were 'believers'. And that they were explaining their philosophy of 'B's' – beers, bananas and Bibles – when Joseph slammed on the brakes and I, along with several Bibles and bananas (I had yet to see any beers), went flying into the dashboard.

When I looked through the windshield there was a flock of camels walking through the yellow headlights, oblivious to us. It took a good two minutes for them to cross the road. I was in the process of smacking myself to try to wake up when Mary explained that camels were brought here before cars and then left to roam the deserts with nothing to do but procreate and now Australia had more wild camels than anywhere on earth.

When the last camel walked off the road ahead it was replaced by an Aboriginal man in jeans and a T-shirt, waving his arms. His clothes, hair and face were caked in red dirt like mine. Behind him was a small station wagon, and next to that a woman, also covered in desert, holding a backpack. The car, other than being upside down, looked just fine. Joseph and Mary rolled their windows up and locked their doors.

Ten minutes later Freddie and his mother-in-law Awoonga were sitting on either side of me as we jiggled along the road. We left their car where it was. Like Joseph and Mary, they had avoided hitting the camels, and, like me, they had knocked over a tree. They'd been travelling from Awoonga's family's farm to Freddie's farm. Both farms were about 400 kilometres from this road on different sides of it. I asked them what they grew and they looked at me oddly. They said they had met a Canadian like me once down in Perth. I told them I was American. Freddie asked me how the black people were in America. I told him they were fine. He asked if their situation was like his. I told him that the predicament of the Native Americans was more like that of the Aborigines. He asked me the same question again. When I didn't respond he asked me to ask his mother-in-law if she had remembered to bring the tomato sauce in her bag. He explained that tribal law forbade them to speak to each other. I asked him why. That was just the way it was, he said. We should all be so lucky, I said. After I asked her, Awoonga said the tomato sauce was on the back of Freddie's shirt. She said it had exploded all over the car and it had made her very scared because she thought it was her insides. Freddie swore under his breath in some language I couldn't understand, then asked if Mary had any tomato sauce. She said no, sorry, and gave us all bananas. Ten minutes later we pulled up to a small tin-roofed house adjoining an enormous garage, all by itself on the side of the road.

'Told you there was a town here,' said Joseph.

At least the lights were on. He pulled alongside the house and said they'd sleep here in the campervan for the night. Freddie, Awoonga and I stepped out, walked up to the front door and knocked.

A couple of minutes later a woman opened the door, screamed and slammed it shut. Another minute passed and a small man came to the door.

'Where in the death of Adam are your clothes, mate?' he asked me. His jaw was so slight and his chin so long it turned his face into a triangle.

I explained the situation and he asked what in the death of Adam that had to do with my clothes. Before I could think of an answer he asked if that was Cyndi Lauper. 'I love that song,' he said. '*I wanna be the one to walk in the sun. Oh girls just wanna have fu-un!*'

I asked if he might be able to work on my van and get Freddie's and work on that too. He informed me that he was watching the Tri-State Rugby Championship and that his wife was the mechanic but she too was watching the Tri-State Rugby Championship and they'd have to do it in the morning and he'd met a Canadian in Melbourne last year and we were very nice people. I said thank you.

'See any dead roos on the way in?' he asked.

'There were a couple kangaroos,' I said. 'I think there was one a few k's south.'

'Puffed up yet, was it?'

'Not really.'

'Bang on. Need to feed the chooks out back. Julia'll grab it in the morning when she gets your mate's ute.'

I thanked him.

Freddie just stood there, staring at the small man.

Finally the man said, 'What is it, blackfella?'

Freddie cleared his throat. 'Do you have any tomato sauce?' he asked.

'G'night.' And the small man closed the door.

On the other side of the road Freddie and I dug a small pit in the hard earth. While we scavenged for firewood he told me about a large rock fish named Alakitja who swam between endless white water lilies in the river known as the Milky Way. The lilies were so bright you could see them from the earth. 'Stars,' said Freddie as he picked up another handful of twigs for kindling. 'While hiding from the hard sun, Alakitja was caught by two brothers and they sit up there now eating him by their campfire which is also named the Southern Cross.' He pointed to it.

The entire band of the Milky Way, which isn't as clearly visible in the Northern Hemisphere, arched overhead from horizon to horizon. Although I had never spotted it, I knew from the Australian flag that the Southern Cross was five stars and I did not understand how you could draw two brothers eating at a campfire out of five points, and I had no idea which stars he was pointing to but I told him they were nice. He tossed the kindling in the pit we had dug and began to cry. I told him they were better than nice, beautiful. He said it was not that. Then he walked off to a tree and I heard branches snapping off it. For the first time, my left foot began to hurt pretty bad.

Once we had the fire going, Awoonga joined us. As did a peacock, but I seemed to be the only one surprised by its presence. Its head drooped and it ignored us and looked very tired but happy to be warm. Freddie dug through Awoonga's backpack, pulled out something the size of a subway sandwich and unwrapped the tinfoil around it. I told him it looked gross, like a cow's tongue or something, and he said that was what it was. He cut it in three pieces and gave one to me and one to Awoonga.

'Sweet, eh?' he said, biting off a decent-sized chunk. 'If only we had tomato sauce. If only.'

It was sinewy but broke apart easily once you really got to chewing it. Like you'd imagine your own tongue probably would if you had the guts to really truly chew on it. And he was right, it would have been better with tomato sauce.

He asked where I was going and I explained that I'd spent four weeks driving around the country and was now headed to Sydney to meet my girlfriend. I asked him if he had a girl.

'I have three wives,' he said. 'But I only have love for one.' He nodded towards Awoonga. 'Her daughter Wangara.'

Awoonga smiled. 'I have not seen her in one year,' she said. 'Freddie is taking me back to his farm in his new car to see her.'

'It is true about loving Wangara,' said Freddie. 'I am not just saying it. I love her ever since she come to our place with Awoonga when she was eight years old and me ten. We would sleep on the floor next to our mattress so that we could listen for the Sun Woman. You see, the Sun Woman rises in the morning and lights a fire below the horizon and there she uses red ochre powder to decorate her face. Often it spills into the air and this is the red of dawn. She goes west to her other campsite and carries her torch, our sun, across the sky. The campsite is just below the horizon and there she smothers the torch and takes off the make-up she uses and it rises again into the air and creates the colours of dusk. To return to her morning camp she walks through a tunnel underground and everything is dark.

'It is an old tale. But me and Wangara would lie on the floor and listen for the Sun Woman in her tunnel. We would lie across from each other and look at each other in the starlight through the open window until starlight went away and the Sun Woman put on her make-up and only then could you see the five gold spots like the Southern Cross in Wangara's left eye that trembled each time she shifted her sight from one of my eyes to the other and the sun came into the room through the window on the wall then down onto the floor making our feet warm as it went higher in the sky and then over our bodies until it went into our eyes and we had to close them and not look at each other any more and only then did we sleep. I love her ever since then and many many suns afterward I still love her and the gold spots in her left eye.'

Joseph came up to the fire and handed each of us a paper cup. 'Banana oatmeal chocolate stout.' He pointed to the small trailer behind the camper. 'Our brewery,' he said. 'Happy Independence Day!'

'Whose independence is it?' I asked.

'Yours,' he said. 'Isn't yours July fourth?'

'Didn't realise it was July,' I said.

I used the beer to wash down the last bit of tongue. The drink was thick as tar, but sweet. Joseph said he had better climb back into bed with Mary but he had two extra sleeping bags in the campervan. Awoonga went with him to get them.

Freddie glared at the fire across from me, his eyes like twin embers. His hair shot straight back, wiry and thick, grey and black like smoke. He sipped his beer. 'What are you doing out here, Josh?' he asked.

'Looking for nothing.'

'Nothing?'

'Well, you see, New Haven – it's a city in the States – is the smallest place I ever lived. Finding a place which is empty, where there is nothing, is everything to me. I drove across the American desert last summer only to find the roads paved and the land fenced off. So I thought I'd give your country a go.'

'You should come to work for me on the farm.'

'What do you grow there?'

'Grow? It is a farm.'

I let it drop.

'Car accidents happen quite often here,' he said.

'No kidding.'

'I was in another one last month.' He lifted his shirt to reveal a bruised and glistening tangle of flesh below the left side of his ribs. 'The gear-shifter did this. It speared me. But, Wangara, her face smashed, she died. I have not been able to tell Awoonga – or have someone tell Awoonga – this. None of her farm knows. But tomorrow we will be at my farm where everyone knows.'

Awoonga walked back into the glow of the fire. She sat beside Freddie and lay the sleeping bags between them. Freddie looked up from his beer to me. His eyes were welling up, the fire's reflection building in the bottoms, the tops white with starlight, and in between his pupils filled with bottomless supplication. Cyndi Lauper, mid-chorus, came to an abrupt halt. There was only the fire. There was none of the insect noises I had heard in other parts of Australia.

I said goodnight, but Freddie was silent, unblinking, afraid to knock those twin reflections down his cheeks. The peacock stuck its head up as I passed it and entered the cold starlight. I crossed the road and opened the back of the panel van and crept onto my mattress. Everything I had was in pieces around me, bathed in dirt the colour of dawn. I put my ear to the floor and heard the Sun Woman's footsteps move further and further away, and waited for sleep until she lit her torch. It looked like dusk. Just on the other side of the road.

THE FIRST HOUR OF THE FIRST DAY OF MY FIRST ASSIGNMENT FOR LONELY PLANET

MILES RODDIS

Despite his distressing first day with Lonely Planet, Miles has gone on to write or contribute to more than 30 Lonely Planet guidebooks. Continuing to cut his teeth on African titles, he covered a band south of the Sahara from Ghana and Burkina Faso to Ethiopia, Eritrea and little Djibouti. Nowadays rather less nimble and altogether broader in girth, he contributes to Mediterranean country, regional and city guides for France, Spain and Italy – plus a refreshing trip north of the Arctic Circle to research Norway.

'The First Hour of the First Day...' © Lonely Planet 2009.

IT'S NOT EASY TO WEDGE your big toe through Lonely Planet's door, knowing full well that every month dozens of other aspirant travel writers are trying to do just the same. So when you're finally granted an assignment, you don't bargain, wheedle and assert your preference for Bhutan, Bali or a few of the more laid-back Caribbean islands.

Thus it was that I found myself on an Air France jumbo, wedged between a Belgian agricultural engineer of mastodon proportions and a mammoth Congolese student heading home after studies in Paris. The night flight had left me terminally jet-lagged, my head awhirl with a thousand and more details from the previous Lonely Planet writer's lowdown. And, as my soggy brain managed to tell me, I was decidedly wet behind the ears from much more than the predawn shave and cold water which I'd sluiced over my face in an attempt to shake myself out of a deep torpor.

I squinted through the plane's porthole as it began its descent towards Bangui airport. Before you reach for your atlas – as I had done, barely a couple of weeks earlier – I'll tell you; it's the capital of the Central African Republic, abbreviated in everyday speech to CAR. Or rather, it's what remains of the capital. The CAR army at that time had a distressing tendency to march unan-nounced out of their barracks, shooting from hip and howitzer to wreak their impressive worst on the town.

The Central African Republic and Chad – the one subject to regular army putsches, the other seemingly engaged in perpetual civil war; such were my first two experiences of life writing for Lonely Planet. Only in retrospect, much later, did I realise the collective sigh of editorial relief that must have wafted through the company's Melbourne office at the news that some mug had at last been signed up to cover the two countries.

Bangui, the few friends who had heard of the place assured me, rivalled Lagos, Nairobi and Abidjan in the quality and quantity of its urban violence. In the words of the very guidebook which I'd been commissioned to update, 'Bangui is a city of thieves and

103

pickpockets. Stay clear of groups of young men. If you go out at night, never walk.'

Welcome to Bangui. As the jumbo began its swoop over the town's small airport, I picked out the armoured cars flanking the runway, each with its platoon of French soldiers wearing a khaki version of those briefest of thigh-hugging shorts that only the French still go in for these days. And each with a large gun mounted and trained towards the skies.

More gun-toting, short-shorts-sporting *soldats* patrolled the arrivals area, where the customs officer discreetly signalled to me that if I equally discreetly made a modest unreceipted payment to his companion, my backpack would pass through without inspection. I affected incomprehension and, in their need to work quickly and profitably through the queue of travellers at my back, they waved me through. Ha! A first tiny triumph.

Few are the travellers who manage the journey between airport and town in Third World countries without being savagely ripped off. But, armed with my guidebook, I knew the reasonable tariff and came out guns blazing, ready for a spot of hard bargaining. Funny that, I mused, as the most assertive taxi driver pulled his battered vehicle away from the arrivals area; funny that I couldn't get a single driver to budge below four times the top rate the guidebook had quoted.

Many are the travellers at airports throughout the world who, because of the persuasive powers of their commission-hungry taxi driver, fetch up at a hotel other than the one of their choice. But I was made of sterner stuff. 'Hôtel Minerva,' I insisted, mindful of Lonely Planet's assessment: 'the only hotel which might possibly be within your price range'.

'*N'existe plus, chef,*' insisted my driver. It's not there any more.

I affected incomprehension once again and, in the manner of tourists when ill at ease, repeated my injunction a couple of decibels louder. '*HÔTEL MINERVA, s'il vous PLAÎT,*' I responded, with both confidence and that ingratiating 'please' which we British feel obliged to append to any order.

'*Y'en a pas, chef.*' No such thing, boss.

Barely 10 minutes and one excessively fat cab fare later (the taxi charge inflated even higher since the driver had no change for the smallest of the large-denomination French banknotes I was carrying), we pulled up outside the Hôtel Minerva. Or rather, outside the remains of the Hôtel Minerva, shot to smithereens by the army in one of its more dramatic sorties.

'*Te l'avais bien dit, chef,*' remarked the driver with a cheery leer, 'told you so. But I know another, much better, special price. This time, the ride's on me.'

Thus it was that, pausing only to note the need to revise my predecessor's assessment of the one-time Hôtel Minerva, I fetched up in a hotel so expensive as to be way beyond consideration for Lonely Planet's *Africa on a Shoestring* – or indeed of any but the most profligate travel writer.

I patiently waited my turn until the protracted negotiations between the receptionist and my driver over his commission were concluded, apparently to neither party's satisfaction. The latter headed mumbling for the street clutching a wad of grimy notes which the former had produced from under the desk. I resisted the receptionist's resistible offer to sell me a dog-eared copy of the collected thoughts of the dead and discredited Emperor Bokassa for the equivalent of a mere US$60. I also registered the fact that I appeared to be the hotel's only guest and, more urgently, that Bangui was about to embark upon three days of national holiday; shops and banks were closing imminently and I hadn't a single Central African franc to my name.

In the privacy of my room, I hurriedly peeled off a few high-denomination French banknotes, scribbled a quick shopping list, grabbed my passport, rammed everything into my pockets and dashed for the door. Heedful of that warning about crime levels, I walked briskly and purposefully in the direction of item 68 on my map of downtown Bangui, side vision keen and mindful of my back.

Hugging the very middle of the muddy, traffic-free road, I

began to get a grip on the town. I noted en passant that item 62, Novotel Bangui, was but a shell; No 54, a modest grocery store, had been torched; and No 61, the Pharmacie Centrale, was gutted. More worryingly, only the twisted girders of item 56, the BCAD bank, remained as witness of the army's latest rampage. And all this since the last Lonely Planet edition and the one I was here to revise.

But amid the destruction, item 68, the solid concrete mass of the BEAC bank, was reassuringly intact, if you ignored a pockmark or two. I mounted its crowded steps, squeezed my way in and picked a passage to the foreign exchange counter, before which, with barely 10 minutes to closing time, an attempt at a queue seethed and swelled.

I briefly assessed my position. Here I stood, profoundly jetlagged, overheated, pasty mouthed, knowing not a soul in town and without a single centime in local currency. Stuck at the end of the scrum, the only non-national in line, my chances of getting any cash were receding with each tick of those 10 minutes. With everyone else about to go on extended holiday, I was preparing to begin a job I'd never done before. Why the hell was I here? I asked myself.

A kind Centrafricain interrupted this self-indulgent reverie, beckoning to me and insisting, despite my half-hearted protestations, that I should slip in front of him, so gaining several places over the mildly protesting back markers.

The mass surged up to and around the window, behind which sat a particularly surly teller. Snarling at the crowd, he would occasionally and arbitrarily grab a paper from the hand of one of the insurgents as the wave of people passed before his booth. But my new-found friend graciously protected me with his body, propelling me gently forward and remonstrating with his compatriots. Whispering the while into my ear his regrets at their uncouthness, he wished me greater good fortune during the rest of my stay as an honoured guest in his country.

Finally, one of the surges propelled me in front of the window, which I grabbed to prevent myself being swept back by the ebb. The teller snatched my passport and I knew that I'd entered the system, that money might well be mine and that I could temporarily relax.

As I turned to thank my protector for his solicitousness towards a visitor, I saw him heading at speed for the main exit. I reached instinctively for my back pocket – and found it empty, the button dexterously flicked open.

It remains one of the great regrets of my life that I wasn't present to celebrate with my erstwhile protector when he opened his fist to reveal – nothing more and nothing less than my shopping list.

THE SIGHTS OF PRAGUE

DANNY WALLACE

Danny Wallace is a comedy writer and producer. He has written three books, including *Yes Man,* which was recently made into a film by Warner Bros, starring Jim Carrey. He lives in London with a girl and no cats.

YOU CAN CALL IT whatever you like.

You can call it a hunch. You can call it instinct. Some might call it a well-honed eye for detail, carved by experience and years on the road – while others might go so far as to call it some kind of secret sixth sense.

But let me tell you, I *knew* something wasn't right about my trip to Prague when the stranger who picked me up at the airport reached under the front seat of the car and pulled out a semi-automatic machine gun.

'It is Uzi 9mm!' he said, grinning at me in that special way that only men holding Uzi 9mms so often do. 'It is good, solid. But…*dangerous.*'

I nodded, and tried a vague smile. To be honest, I'd already *guessed* that an Uzi 9mm was probably a bit dangerous, despite the fact that I'd never seen one before, let alone been shown one by a bald Eastern European in a car. Maybe I *do* have a sixth sense, after all.

I had flown to Prague at the last minute to write a piece for a music magazine. An up-and-coming British band happened to be playing in town, and I'd been asked to cover the gig. I'd said yes straightaway – this would be my first chance to see Prague, and the trip would include several hours where I'd have nothing to do. I could see the sights, get a feel for the place, go to the gig and come home. I'd be meeting the photographer in a couple of hours, in the centre of Prague. But that was only if I made it that far.

I'd been told I'd be picked up by a local driver called Honza, a friend-of-a-friend of the man who usually picked people up – and here he was, holding his Uzi 9mm with a grin. I grinned back. Now we were just two men in a small white car, grinning at each other – one of them armed.

'You want Uzi 9mm?' he asked.

'I'm fine for Uzi 9mms,' I said, quite honestly. I could only hope that by offering me an Uzi 9mm, Honza wasn't also challenging me to a duel.

111

'I mean, to hold?' he said. 'You want hold gun?'

He was looking at me with what seemed to be real hope in his eyes. I didn't quite know what to say. I didn't really want to hold the gun, but being British, I didn't want to *not* hold it either, in case by not holding this man's gun I made him feel uncomfortable or offended him in any way. As a well-raised Briton, I find it difficult to refuse anybody anything they might want whatsoever. This is also, incidentally, why I tend to avoid the gay nightclub scene.

'Okay then,' I said, slowly, 'I will hold the gun.'

He passed the weapon to me, his face aglow, and I held it for a moment. It was heavy and metal. That's all I can tell you. I was, it seems, never destined to be a reviewer for *Guns 'n' Ammo*.

'You like?' asked Honza, eagerly.

'It is brilliant,' I replied, handing it back almost immediately.

'Okay!' said Honza. 'Now we go!'

Honza tucked the Uzi under his seat, and reached into his pocket for something. I figured so long as it wasn't a hand grenade, I'd be happy.

It was a knife.

A knife that he then jammed, with some considerable speed and force, into the ignition of the car. He twisted it once, and the car roared into life. We sped out of the airport car park so quickly that for a moment I wished for the safe old days, when we were just two strangers, in a foreign country, playing with guns.

'So, um, why exactly do you have a gun under your seat?' I asked, after a silent ten minutes or so.

'Ah,' said Honza, sadly. 'To protect. Local gangs, mafia people. Some bad gypsy people, too. They look for tourist, or foreigner. They steal list of people flying into Czech, and then they make a small sign with name on, and stand at airport and wait for you. They bribe real driver away. And then they take you out of city, to country, and rob you with gun.'

'Oh,' I said, slightly relieved.

Until I realised that Honza had met me at the airport with a small sign with 'Mr Wallace' written on it, and that Honza had a gun, and that outside the window of the car, the grey of the city was instead becoming the green of the countryside...

It turned out, of course, that Honza was not about to rob me. He just had a few errands to run before he could drop me off in town. I mean, of *course* he did. When else would you run errands but when you've been asked to pick up a British journalist from the airport? You certainly don't do them before you've picked him up, as that would be a waste of valuable time, and you don't do them afterwards, do you, because then you'd get home late. No, no. You wait until you've picked him up, and then you spend nearly an hour and a half driving around the Czech Republic picking up bags of plant pots from women in floral dresses and getting your windscreen washed by a dusty minor. Then, and *only* then, do you take the journalist to his destination, which, in this case, was a pub. Still, I didn't mind too much. So I wasn't going to see Prague straightaway. I could see it later – after I'd met the photographer or after the gig.

The photographer who was supposed to be waiting for me in the pub was not, of course, waiting for me in the pub.

At first, I didn't mind too much. Surely he'd be along in a minute or two. Perhaps he was off buying film. Maybe one of his flashbulbs had broken. There was still time. The gig didn't start for a few hours, and he was only a little bit late.

Honza had decided to park the car and come inside with me. He even said he was going to come along with me to the gig. So together we sat, awaiting the arrival of the photographer, and nursing two inordinately cheap pints of beer. I'd hoped that at least our rendezvous point would be an example of proper, old-fashioned Czechoslovakia. It wasn't. The main clue was its name: Mulligans. There were other clues, too – the bicycle bolted to the wall and the giant plastic bearded leprechaun being just two of them. It appeared that we were sitting in an Irish theme pub designed by someone who had never actually been to Ireland.

This was back in the late nineties, when Prague seemed on the cusp of huge commercial change – that is, it was gracelessly changing from a priceless fairy-tale village to a city entirely sponsored by McDonald's.

It was this aspect of Prague that I was rather pompously contemplating (I do, after all, live in London – a city that proudly claims as one of its main tourist attractions a big neon sign with the word 'Fuji' written on it), when a stranger sat down next to us.

He was scruffy, unkempt and reeked strongly of whisky. In other words, he looked like he was probably the photographer.

'This is Jiri,' said Honza. 'He is butcher.'

It wasn't the photographer.

I raised my hand in greeting, and would have said hello had I not then immediately remembered my encounter with the Uzi. I found myself hoping that 'Butcher' was this man's occupation, as opposed to his nickname.

Jiri looked at me and smiled, then uttered a sentence which impressed me as much for its speed and confidence as it did for its total and utter lack of any discernible vowels. Not able to speak Czech, I blinked at the man a couple of times, and said, 'Um…'

'American?' he said. 'British?'

'British,' said Honza.

'What you are doing here? Holidays?'

'No,' I said. 'I'm just waiting for someone.'

'Who you are waiting for?' said Jiri. 'Tony Blair?'

And then he laughed and laughed and laughed, smacking the table with the palm of his hand, and turned to Honza, who was also laughing. Then they both stopped laughing and looked at me.

'No,' I said, quite calmly. 'I am not waiting for Tony Blair. That would be ludicrous. I am waiting for a photographer.'

Jiri brought his hand to his chest.

'I am photographer,' he said.

I blinked again.

'Are you?' I queried.

'No,' he said. 'I am not photographer. I am butcher.'

'Oh.'

I couldn't help but wonder what had prompted Jiri to play such an elaborate hoax on me.

'But!' he said. 'I have camera!'

At this, Honza and Jiri started to talk very excitedly in Czech. And then Honza got out of his seat and said, 'I come back soon.'

I looked at my watch. There was still no sign of the photographer. Perhaps he wanted me to meet him at the gig. I reached into my pocket and tried to find the piece of paper on which I'd written the name of the venue. Jiri watched me do this, then leaned forward, conspiratorially.

'What do you want, my friend?' he whispered, his eyes darting nervously around the room.

'How do you mean?' I asked, confused.

'Anything you want, I can get you. You are friend of Honza, you are friend of my. What do you want?'

I thought about it, and shrugged. Perhaps he thought I wanted a tour guide, which, come to think of it, wasn't such a bad idea.

'You want to smoke something? I can get you something. Anything I can get you, in Praha it is all possible. You want class A, I get you class A.'

Oh good God. The Butcher was trying to sell me illegal substances, when all I wanted was an hour to myself and someone to tell me where all the pretty buildings were. First I'm picked up by an armed stranger, and now I'm sitting underneath a bright-green leprechaun with a criminal butcher who wants to find something he can sell me.

'A girl? You want a girl? I get you girls. Anything you want, my friend, it is possible.'

'To be honest, I'm okay at the moment...'

'A gun?'

'No!' I said. 'No, I don't want a gun. Or a girl. Or any Class As...'

Jiri leaned back in his chair, cast his eyes round the room, and then leaned forward again. 'Anti-tank missile?'

Anti-tank missile?!

'Whatever it is,' he said, 'it all can happen. It can take time, yes, but...'

'Um, look...'

'Ah!' he said, suddenly, pointing a finger in the air. 'You want Chicago Bull? I can get you Chicago Bull!'

'*Chicago Bull?* What's a Chicago Bull?'

But the truth was, I didn't *want* to know. I had a hunch he was referring to something illicit and dodgy, but to be honest, even if he was referring to the basketball team itself, I wouldn't have been interested. There is a time and a place for illegally purchasing massive, millionaire basketball players, and the corner table of an Irish pub in Prague isn't it.

'Really,' I said. 'I am absolutely fine for all the things you have mentioned. Even the anti-tank missile and the Chicago Bull, whatever that is. I am simply waiting for the photographer to arrive and then we are going to go and see some music.'

Honza walked back into the pub just then, and Jiri put his finger to his lips, willing me not to let on about his minor indiscretions, such as drug dealing, pimping and the potential kidnap of some nine-foot sportsmen.

'I have camera,' said Honza, placing a small and battered disposable Kodak camera on the table. 'Now we go.'

'*You're* the photographer?' I asked, as we drove over the Charles Bridge, heading for the gig. '*You?*'

'No. I am not photographer. But photographer did not come tonight. So I help you. We have camera, what is problem?'

We were alone again now. Jiri had stayed on at the pub and given me a knowing wink as I walked out the door, mouthing what I *think* were the words 'grenade launcher'.

'We go Dlouhá,' said Honza, and I nodded, even though I didn't know what he was saying. I was growing a little nervous now. I'd been told the venue was only moments away from the pub, but already we seemed to have been driving for a lot longer and in what I irrationally believed to be the wrong direction. Plus, the photographer was missing. Oh my God, the photographer was *missing*. He was probably *dead*! He'd clearly got to the pub early and run into the Butcher. Or maybe Honza had got to him earlier today with his Uzi...

'How much you paying photographer?' said Honza.

'I don't know. The magazine was paying him.'

Honza made an odd grumbling sound. We were thundering over a cobbled street now and into a square, where trams were stopping and people dashed through slanting rain.

Honza slowed to a halt. 'There it is. You go in, I follow.'

And I did as he said.

The band came on half an hour late to mild and scattered applause from a bored-looking audience. But they played well and won the crowd over, and soon the place was rocking. I looked around, trying to catch a glimpse of anyone with a camera, anyone who might be the guy I was supposed to meet. But there was only Honza – clutching his disposable camera in one hand and a beer in the other and clicking away from the back of the room. I made a few notes and drank a bottle of water. And then the gig was over.

'I only make seven photograph,' said Honza, back by my side. 'Already this camera was full.'

'I'm sure that'll be fine,' I said, eager to get away, to finally be free. 'Thank you very much for that.'

There was an awkward silence.

'Well,' I said, offering Honza my hand, hoping that this would be the moment I could make a break and flee into the night to see all that Prague had to offer.

'And now we eat!' said Honza.

An hour later we were sitting in a fine little restaurant, chewing bread and meat and drinking beer. A few of Honza's friends had turned up, and although I couldn't understand them, the atmosphere was warm as we sat there and laughed and drank and laughed some more.

I suddenly felt quite guilty. I mean, this wasn't so bad, was it? So I wasn't exactly seeing Prague – but maybe, by hanging out with the locals, I was experiencing a more important Prague, the Prague of the people.

I looked over to Honza. 'You like the food?' he asked. 'Good food, huh?' I nodded, and realised something shocking. I had clearly jumped to some very wrong conclusions about this man. He hadn't *needed* to invite me out. He hadn't *needed* to fetch his camera and take pictures of the band. He was a genuinely nice, hospitable and friendly man. Someone who was only supposed to pick me up from the airport, but who was now spending all evening looking after me. Just because he had a gun in his car and his friend had tried to sell me black-market weaponry didn't necessarily make him a bad person.

As I accepted another beer from this table of strangers, I resolved to be less judgemental in the future. I'd learned an important lesson, and if someone tries to sell you black-market weaponry one day, I hope you'll remember my experience in Prague and not think too badly of them.

'Here, Danny,' said Honza, holding a small shot glass filled to the brim with something green. 'Drink!'

I downed the shot to the cheers of the table, and we ordered another.

'Tonight, Danny, you stay with me,' said Honza.

'No, no,' I said. 'It's okay. I've got a hotel booked.'

'Which hotel?'

'It's called Hotel Pyramid, or something.'

'No, no – that is terrible! You stay with me. Please!'

'But it's booked!'

'We unbook it. You stay with me!'

And I looked around the table at the smiling faces and said humbly, 'Thank you, Honza.'

When the bill finally came I suddenly realised that I hadn't had time to change any money yet. Honza just smiled and waved my objections away, and the bill was paid. I smiled. What genuinely lovely people.

A few of us went back to Honza's that night, and as the clock edged towards 3am, I fell asleep, drunk and happy, on the sofa in the living room.

Four hours later I was being shaken awake.

'Danny! Come! We must leave!'

It was Honza.

'Eh?'

'We must leave now! We go!'

'Where?'

'To the airport!'

He was smiling the broadest smile I think I have ever seen.

'But it's only seven in the morning! My flight isn't until two.'

'I have things I must do.'

'I'll get a taxi to the airport later on. I want to see some of Prague anyway. I still haven't managed to see it.'

'I show you sights in car,' said Honza. 'Please, we leave now.'

Confused and tired, I quietly got my things together.

I'm not sure what sights normal tourists get to see when they visit Prague. I'm told they're entranced by the majesty of the old town. I'm told they stand and stare for hours before the gates of the mighty castle. I'm told some fall in love with St Nicholas Cathedral, while others never want to leave the Old Gardens. Evidently, Honza didn't think any of these were the slightest bit important. Which is why most of what I saw of Prague was a motorway, a brewery and the back of Jiri's block of flats. Honza had more errands to run – the very last of which, it turned out, was dropping me off at the airport.

I began to thank him for looking after me in such a – well – *unusual* way, but he had one last thing to say.

'This is for you,' he said, and handed me an envelope. I was touched. Honza had obviously written me a letter, thanking me for my friendship and wishing me the best. Or perhaps it was the photos, which he'd secretly had developed as a parting gift. Or maybe it was an invitation to come back sometime, to enjoy more of his generous hospitality.

I opened it. It was a bill.

Car. Drinks. Photos.

I couldn't quite believe it.

Meal.

I was being charged for the meal? And not just for *my* meal, either. It seemed I was being asked to pay for *everyone's!*

Hotel.

He was calling his sofa a hotel?

Prague Tour.

Prague Tour?! A brewery and the back of his mate's house!

I was dumbstruck, and not a little vexed.

I looked at Honza, who looked at me and smiled. I remembered the Uzi under his seat. And the knife in the ignition. It was all I could do not to scour the horizon for Jiri and an anti-tank missile.

And so I bravely said, 'I only have British money on me.'

'Okay,' said Honza.

Twenty minutes later I stood in the check-in queue and considered the fact that my trip to Prague had actually cost me more than I had earned. And then I looked up and caught a glimpse of bald, beefy Honza walking towards the arrivals area, carrying a small sign that read 'Mr Thomas'.

Mr Thomas, if you are reading this, please get in touch. It would be nice to reminisce about all the things we saw in wonderful, unforgettable Prague.

CITY OF DJINNS
WILLIAM DALRYMPLE

William Dalrymple is a Fellow of the Royal Society of Literature and of the Royal Asiatic Society, and in 2002 was awarded the Mungo Park Medal by the Royal Scottish Geographical Society for his 'outstanding contribution to travel literature'. He wrote and presented the TV series *Stones of the Raj* and *Indian Journeys,* which won BAFTA's 2002 Grierson Award for Best Documentary Series. He and his wife, artist Olivia Fraser, have three children and divide their time between London and Delhi.

THE FLAT PERCHED at the top of the house, little more than a lean-to riveted to Mrs Puri's ceiling. The stairwell exuded sticky, airless September heat; the roof was as thin as corrugated iron.

Inside we were greeted by a scene from *Great Expectations:* a thick pall of dust on every surface, a family of sparrows nesting in the blinds and a fleece of old cobwebs – great arbours of spider silk – arching the corner walls. Mrs Puri stood at the doorway, a small, bent figure in a *salwar kameez.*

'The last tenant did not go out much,' she said, prodding the cobwebs with her walking stick. She added: 'He was not a tidy gentleman.' Olivia blew on a cupboard; the dust was so thick you could sign your name in it.

Our landlady, though a grandmother, soon proved herself to be a formidable woman. A Sikh from Lahore, Mrs Puri was expelled from her old home during Partition and in the upheavals of 1947 lost everything. She arrived in Delhi on a bullock cart. Forty-two years later she had made the transition from refugee pauper to Punjabi princess. She was now very rich indeed. She owned houses all over Delhi and had swapped her bullock for a fleet of new Maruti cars, the much coveted replacement for the old Hindustan Ambassador. Mrs Puri also controlled a variety of business interests. These included the Gloriana Finishing School, India's first etiquette college, a unique institution which taught village girls how to use knives and forks, apply lipstick and make polite conversation about the weather.

Mrs Puri had achieved all this through a combination of hard work and good old-fashioned thrift. In the heat of summer she rarely put on the air-conditioning. In winter she allowed herself the electric fire for only an hour a day. She recycled the newspapers we threw out; and returning from parties late at night we could see her still sitting up, silhouetted against the window, knitting sweaters for export. 'Sleep is silver,' she would say in explanation, 'but money is gold.'

This was all very admirable, but the hitch, we soon learned, was that she expected her tenants to emulate the disciplines she imposed upon herself. One morning, after only a week in the flat, I turned on the tap to discover that our water had been cut off, so went downstairs to sort out the problem. Mrs Puri had already been up and about for several hours; she had been to the gurdwara, said her prayers and was now busy drinking her morning glass of rice water.

'There is no water in our flat this morning, Mrs Puri.'

'No, Mr William, and I am telling you why.'

'Why, Mrs Puri?'

'You are having guests, Mr William. And always they are going to the lavatory.'

'But why should that affect the water supply?'

'Last night I counted seven flushes,' said Mrs Puri, rapping her stick on the floor. 'So I have cut off the water as protest.'

She paused to let the enormity of our crime sink in.

'Is there any wonder that there is water shortage in our India when you people are making seven flushes in one night?'

Old Mr Puri, her husband, was a magnificent-looking Sikh gentleman with a long white beard and a tin zimmer frame with wheels on the bottom. He always seemed friendly enough – as we passed he would nod politely from his armchair. But when we first took the flat Mrs Puri drew us aside and warned us that her husband had never been, well, quite the same since the riots that followed Mrs Gandhi's death in 1984.

It was a rather heroic story. When some hooligans began to break down the front door, Mr Puri got Ladoo (the name means Sweety), his bearer, to place him directly behind the splintering wood. Uttering a blood-curdling cry, he whipped out his old service revolver and fired the entire magazine through the door. The marauders ran off to attack the taxi rank around the corner and the Puris were saved.

From that day on, however, the old man had become a fervent Sikh nationalist. 'Everyone should have their own home,' he would snort. 'The Muslims have Pakistan. The Hindus have Hindustan. The Punjab is our home. If I was a young man I would join Bhindranwale and fight these Hindu dogs.'

'It is talk only,' Mrs Puri would reply.

'Before I die I will see a free Khalistan.'

'You are daydreaming only. How many years are left?'

'The Punjab is my home.'

'He may have been born in the Punjab,' Mrs Puri would say, turning to me, 'but now he could not go back to village life. He likes flush toilet and Star TV. Everybody likes flush toilet and Star TV. How can you leave these things once you have tasted such luxury?'

Since the riots, Mr Puri had also become intermittently senile. One day he could be perfectly lucid; the next he might suffer from the strangest hallucinations. On these occasions conversations with him took on a somewhat surreal quality:

MR PURI: (up the stairs to my flat) Mr William! Get your bloody mules out of my room this minute!

WD: But Mr Puri, I don't have any mules.

MR PURI: Nonsense! How else could you get your trunks up the stairs?

During our first month in the flat, however, Mr Puri was on his best behaviour. Apart from twice proposing marriage to my wife, he behaved with perfect decorum.

It had been a bad monsoon. Normally in Delhi, September is a month of almost equatorial fertility and the land seems refreshed and newly-washed. But in the year of our arrival, after a parching summer, the rains had lasted for only three weeks. As a result dust was everywhere and the city's trees and flowers all looked as if they had been lightly sprinkled with talcum powder.

Nevertheless the air was still sticky with damp-heat, and it was in a cloud of perspiration that we began to unpack and to take in the eccentricities of our flat: the chiming doorbell that played both the Indian national anthem and 'Land of Hope and Glory'; the geyser, which if left on too long, would shoot a fountain of boiling water from an outlet on the roof and bathe the terrace in a scalding shower; the pretty round building just below the garden which we at first took to be a temple, and only later discovered to be the local sewage works.

But perhaps the strangest novelty of coming to live in India – stranger even than Mrs Puri – was getting used to life with a sudden glut of domestic help. Before coming out to Delhi we had lived impecuniously in a tiny student dive in Oxford. Now we had to make the transition to a life where we still had only two rooms, but suddenly found ourselves with more than twice that number of servants. It wasn't that we particularly wanted or needed servants; but, as Mrs Puri soon made quite clear, employing staff was a painful necessity on which the prestige of her household depended.

The night we moved in, we spent our first hours dusting and cleaning before sinking, exhausted, into bed at around 2am. The following morning we were woken at 7.30 sharp by 'Land of Hope and Glory'. Half asleep, I shuffled to the door to find Ladoo, Mr Puri's bearer, waiting outside. He was holding a tray. On the tray were two glasses of milky Indian *chai*.

'*Chota hazari, sahib,*' said Ladoo. Bed tea.

'What a nice gesture,' I said returning to Olivia. 'Mrs Puri has sent us up some tea.'

'I wish she had sent it up two hours later,' said Olivia from beneath her sheets.

I finished the tea and sank down beneath the covers. Ten seconds later the Indian national anthem chimed out. I scrambled out of bed and again opened the door. Outside was a thin man with purple, betel-stained lips. He had a muffler wrapped around his head and, despite the heat, a thick donkey-jacket was buttoned tightly over his torso. I had never seen him before.

'*Mali,*' he said. The gardener.

He bowed, walked past me and made for the kitchen. From the bedroom I could hear him fiddling around, filling a bucket with water then splashing it over the plants on the roof terrace. He knocked discreetly on the bedroom door to indicate he had finished, then disappeared down the stairs. The *mali* was followed first by Murti, the sweeper, then by Prasad, the *dhobi,* and finally by Bahadur, Mrs Puri's Nepali cook. I gave up trying to sleep and went downstairs.

'Mrs Puri,' I said. 'There has been a stream of strange people pouring in and out of my flat since seven-thirty.'

'I know, Mr William,' replied Mrs Puri. 'These people are your servants.'

'But I don't want any servants.'

'Everyone has servants,' said Mrs Puri. 'You must have servants too. This is what these people are for.'

I frowned. 'But must we have so many?'

'Well, you must have a cook and a bearer.'

'We don't need a bearer. And both of us enjoy cooking.'

'In that case you could have one cook-bearer. One man, two jobs. Very modern. Then there is the *mali,* the sweeper, and a *dhobi* for your washing. Also you must be having one driver.' Mrs Puri furrowed her brow. 'It is very important to have good chauffeur,' she said gravely. 'Some pukka fellow with a smart uniform.'

'I haven't got a car. So it's pointless having a driver.'

'But if you have no car and no driver,' said Mrs Puri, 'how will you be getting from place to place?'

Balvinder Singh, son of Punjab Singh, Prince of Taxi Drivers, may your moustache never grow grey! Nor your liver cave in with cirrhosis. Nor your precious Hindustan Ambassador ever again crumple in a collision – like the one we had with the van carrying Mango Frooty Drink.

Although during my first year in Delhi I remember thinking that the traffic had seemed both anarchic and alarming, by my second visit I had come to realise that it was in fact governed by very strict rules. Right of way belongs to the driver of the largest vehicle. Buses give way to heavy trucks, Ambassadors give way to buses, and bicyclists give way to everything except pedestrians.

On the road, as in many other aspects of Indian life, Might is Right.

Yet Mr Balvinder Singh is an individualist who believes in the importance of asserting himself. While circumstances may force him to defer to buses and lorries, he has never seen the necessity of giving way to the tinny new Maruti vans which, though taller than his Ambassador, are not so heavily built. After all, Mr Singh is a *kshatriya* by caste, a warrior, and like his ancestors he is keen to show that he is afraid of nothing. He disdains such cowardly acts as looking in wing mirrors or using his indicators. His Ambassador is his chariot, his klaxon his sword. Weaving into the oncoming traffic, playing 'chicken' with the other taxis, Balvinder Singh is a Raja of the Road.

Or rather was. One month after our arrival in Delhi, Mr Singh and I had an accident. Taking a road junction with more phlegm than usual, we careered into the Maruti van, impaling it on its bows, so that it bled Mango Frooty Drink all over Mr Singh's bonnet. No one was hurt, and Mr Singh – strangely elated by his 'kill' – took it stoically. 'Mr William,' he said. 'In my life six times have I crashed. And on not one occasion have I ever been killed.'

Although I am devoted to him, Olivia is quick to point out that Mr Singh is in many ways an unattractive character. A Punjabi Sikh, he is the Essex Man of the East. He chews *paan* and spits the betel juice out of the window, leaving a red 'go-fast' stripe along the car's right flank. He utters incoherent whoops of joy as he drives rickshaws on to the pavement or sends a herd of paper boys flying into a ditch. He leaps out of his taxi to urinate at traffic lights, and scratches his groin as he talks. Like Essex Man, he is a lecher. His eyes follow the saris up and down the Delhi avenues; plump Sikh girls riding side-saddle on motorbikes are a particular distraction. Twice a week, when Olivia is not in the car, he offers to drive me to GB Road, the Delhi red light district: 'Just looking,' he suggests. 'Delhi ladies very good. Having breasts like mangoes.'

Yet he has his principles. Like his English counterpart, he is a believer in hard work. He finds it hard to understand the beggars who congregate at the lights. 'Why these peoples not working?' he asks. 'They have two arms and two legs. They not handicrafted.'

'Handicrafted?'

'Missing leg perhaps, or only one ear.'

'You mean handicapped?'

'Yes. Handicrafted. Sikh peoples not like this. Sikh peoples working hard, earning money, buying car.'

Ignoring the bus hurtling towards us, he turns around and winks an enormous wink. 'Afterwards Sikh peoples drinking whisky, looking television, eating tandoori chicken and going GB Road.'

The house stood looking on to a small square of hot, tropical green: a springy lawn fenced in by a windbreak of champa and ashok trees. The square was the scene for a daily routine of almost Vedic inflexibility.

Early in the morning, under a bald blue sky, the servants would walk plump dachshunds over the grass, or, duties completed, would stand about on the pavements exchanging gossip or playing cards. Then, at about nine o'clock, the morning peace would be broken by a procession of bicycle-powered vendors, each with his own distinctive street-cry: the used-newspaper collector ('Paper-wallah! Paper-wallah! Paper-wallah!') would be followed by the fruit seller ('Mangoes! Lychees! Bananas! Papaya!'), the bread boy and the man with the vegetable barrow. My favourite, the cotton-fluffer, whose life revolved around the puffing up of old mattresses, would twang a Jew's harp. On Sunday mornings an acrobat would come with his dancing bear; he had a pair of drums and when he beat them the whole square would miraculously fill with children. Early that afternoon would follow a blind man with an accordion. He would sing hymns and sacred qawwalis and sometimes the rich people would send down a servant with a handful of change.

In the late afternoon, a herd of cattle 20 or 30 strong could be seen wandering along the lane at the back of the house. There was never any herder in sight, but they would always rumble slowly past, throwing up clouds of dust. Occasionally they would collide with the household servants wobbling along the back lane on their bicycles, returning from buying groceries in Khan Market. Then followed the brief Indian dusk: a pale Camembert sun sinking down to the treeline; the smell of woodsmoke and dung cooking fires; the last raucous outbursts from the parakeets and the brahminy mynas; the first whirring, humming cicadas.

Later on, lying in bed, you could hear the *chowkidars* stomping around outside, banging their sticks and blowing their whistles. There were never any robberies in our part of New Delhi, and the *chowkidars* were an entirely redundant luxury.

But, as Mrs Puri said, you had to keep up appearances.

Mr Singh also had strong views about appearances.

'You are Britisher,' he said, the very first time I hailed him. 'I know you are a Britisher.'

It was late afternoon at the end of our first week in Delhi. We had just moved in and were beginning the gruelling pilgrimage through Indian government departments that all new arrivals must perform. We were late for an appointment at the Foreigners Regional Registration Office, yet Mr Singh's assertion could not go unquestioned.

'How do you know I'm a Britisher?'

'Because,' said Mr Singh, 'you are not sporting.'

'Actually I am quite sporting,' I replied. 'I go for a run every day, swim in the summer…'

'No Britisher is sporting,' said Mr Singh, undaunted.

'Lots of my countrymen are very keen on sport,' I retorted.

'No, no,' said Mr Singh. 'You are not catching me.'

'We are still a force to be reckoned with in the 1500 metres, and sometimes our cricket team…'

'No, no,' said Mr Singh. 'Still you are not catching me. You

Britishers are not *sporting*.' He twirled the waxed curlicues of his moustache. 'All men should be sporting a moustache, because all ladies are liking too much.'

He indicated that I should get in.

'It is the fashion of our days,' he said, roaring off and narrowly missing a pedestrian.

Mr Singh's taxi stand lay behind the India International Centre, after which it took its name: International Backside Taxis. The stand was run by Punjab Singh, Balvinder's stern and patriarchal father, and manned by Balvinder and his two plump brothers, Gurmuck and Bulwan. There was also a rota of cousins who would fill in during the weekends and at nights. Over the following months we got to know them all well, but it was Balvinder who remained our special friend.

IGNORING THE ADMIRAL
JAN MORRIS

Jan Morris, who is Anglo-Welsh and lives in Wales, wrote some 40 books before declaring that *Trieste and the Meaning of Nowhere* (2001) was her best and accordingly would be her last. Since then, though, she has been working upon retrospective selections of her work, and in 2010 WW Norton will publish *Contact!*, a book of personal encounters during her long life of travel.

DEVOTED AS I AM to the ethos of Lonely Planet, I was never a backpacker. 'The British Navy always travels first class,' Admiral of the Fleet, Lord 'Jacky' Fisher used to say as he checked into yet another fashionable spa, and I was similarly conditioned during my adolescent years as an officer with the 9th Queen's Royal Lancers of the British Army. At the end of World War II, when we were not getting messy in our dirty old tanks, we were making sure that we ate at the best restaurants and stayed at the poshest hotels.

Nowhere did we honour Lord Fisher's axiom more loyally than in Venice, where we happily made the most of our status as members of a victorious occupying army. Many of the best hotels became our officers' clubs, while the most expensive restaurants were pleased to accept our vastly inflated currency (which we had very likely acquired by selling cigarettes on the black market). And in particular, since all the city's motorboats had been requisitioned by the military, we rode up and down the Grand Canal, under the Rialto Bridge, over to the Lido, like so many lucky young princes.

That was half a century ago, and I have been back to Venice at least a hundred times since. I have never forgotten Fisher's dictum (although he died, I must tell you, five years before I was born), and until last year I had never once in my life so far neglected it as to take a *vaporetto*, a public water-bus, from the railway station into the centre of the city. There no longer being commandeered motorboats available, I had invariably summoned one of the comfortably insulated and impeccably varnished water-taxis which, for a notoriously extravagant fee, would whisk me without hassle to the quayside of my hotel.

My partner, Elizabeth, had not been subjected to the same influences of adolescence. She spent her wartime years as a rating in the women's naval service, decoding signals in an underground war room, subsisting on baked beans and vile sweet tea from the canteen. But she had been to Venice with me dozens of times and I thought that by now I had initiated her into my own Fisherian style of travel. However, last time we were there she proved unexpectedly recidivist. 'Oh, Jan,' she said as I hastened her towards the line of waiting taxis, ignoring the throbbing *vaporetto* at its pier. 'Why must you always be so extravagant? What's wrong with the *vaporetto*? Everyone else goes on it. It's a fraction of the price. What's the hurry anyway? What are you proving? We're not made of money, you know. What's the point?'

'The British Navy always –' I began, but she interrupted me with an aphorism of her own. 'Waste not, want not,' she primly retorted. Ah well, said I to myself, and to Lord Fisher too, anything for a quiet life. Humping our bags in the gathering dusk, tripping over ourselves, fumbling for the right change, dropping things all over the place, with our tickets between our teeth, we stumbled up the gangplank onto the already jam-packed deck.

There we stood for what felt like three or four days, edging into eternity, while the vessel pounded its way through the darkness up the Grand Canal, stopping at every available jetty with deafening engine-reversals, throwing us about with judderings, clangings and bumps, while we stood cheek-by-jowl with 10,000 others on the cold and windy poop. When at last we debouched on the quayside below San Marco, looking as though we were stepping onto Omaha Beach, Elizabeth turned to me with an air of satisfaction. 'There you are, you see. That wasn't so bad, was it? Think of the money we saved! After all these years, I bet you'll never take one of those exorbitant taxis again. A penny saved is a penny gained.'

But she spoke this meaningless maxim too late. Pride, I nearly told her, comes before a fall. Standing there upon the quayside slung about with bags and surrounded by suitcases, I had already discovered that during our ride on the *vaporetto* somebody had stolen the wallet that contained all our worldly wealth, not to mention all our credit cards. Off we trudged to the police station to report the loss, and as we sat in the dim light among a melancholy little assembly of unfortunates and ne'er-do-wells, how I regretted ignoring the Admiral! I bet Elizabeth did too, although she was too proud to admit it.

I didn't actually say 'Penny wise, pound foolish'. I didn't even murmur under my breath the bit about travelling first class. Never hit a woman when she's down, I told myself. Virtue is its own reward – and as it happened, it was rewarded. We never got that wallet back, but the *carabinieri* were terribly solicitous, and said how sorry they were, and assured us that no Venetian could have done such a thing – it must have been one of those Albanians – and sent us off feeling perfectly comforted and a little bit sorry for *them*, actually, so palpable was their sense of civic shame.

Half an hour later, feeling emotionally and physically drained, we turned up on the doorstep of Harry's Bar, a hostelry I have frequented ever since those glory days of victory, when I was young and easy, as the poet said, and Time let me hail and climb. With Jack Fisher beside us – he would have loved Harry's Bar – we pushed our way through the revolving door and told our sad story to the people inside.

And lo! They gave us a free dinner (scampi and white wine, with a zabaglione afterwards) just to cheer us up. For once our truisms did not conflict. Every cloud, we agreed, as the three of us sat there in the warmth of our first-class corner, really does have a silver lining.

THE QUEST
KAREN LEE BOREN

Karen Lee Boren's fiction and nonfiction has appea red in journals and anthologies, including the *Flori da Review, Night Train, Karamu, Hawai'i Pacific Review, Dominion Review, Yemassee, Epoch, Cream City Review, Bookforum* and *Fourth Genre*. Her novel *Girls in Peril* was selected for the Barnes & Noble Discover Great New Writers Award series. She has completed writing residencies at Norcroft, the Millay Colony for the Arts, Blue Mountain Artists Center and Virginia Center for the Creative Arts. She is an associate professor at Rhode Island College and has just completed a novel titled *Month of Fire*.

FROM THE OUTSIDE, the London Quest Hotel did not seem fantastic, or even particularly interesting. It crouched amiably amidst the seediness of Earl's Court, an area of London known as 'Down Under' because of the abundance of Aussie and Kiwi youths who lived there while working to earn money to 'do' Europe. The Kiwi woman who sat next to me on the train from Dover to Victoria Station told me in her clipped accent that the Quest was cheap, clean ('if you're not one of them picky Americans'), and would do until I could find some work. I scoffed with her at my pernickety compatriots, certain that after a month in France of sleeping on night trains and showering in railway stations, if at all, I had sloughed off any inherited hygienic preoccupations. More importantly, I knew that after yet another plummet of the dollar and no work permit in hand, I didn't have the luxury of being fastidious.

I had an address and vague directions, but like most places in London, the Quest was still difficult to find. As I walked the length of Earl's Court Road, I played the London match game, trying to find street signs that corresponded with the wild maps in my *London A to Z*. Both my pack and my spirits were heavy and more than a little damp from the cold, steady mist, so when I turned onto Pembroke Road and saw the green-and-white sign grandly declaring *The London Quest Hotel*, I made the rash decision to stay there no matter how decrepit it turned out to be.

The price for a bed was six pounds per night, so an Australian woman with a ruddy face told me. As though refusing to believe that November could be anything but spring, she wore a tight Lycra tank top exposing the massive flesh of her arms, shoulders and upper back. Her buoyant breasts looked as though they might happily nourish triplets. Thrusting her fingers through the brass bars that made up the upper half of the reception door, she handed me a slip of paper on which the house rules were written. I looked at her bulky frame shoved into this tiny closet, and found myself feeling the same mixture of rage and sadness I felt at the zoo when I saw an animal housed in a pen too small for it to do anything but sit and stare gloomily at the crowds of people that filed past. But she didn't seem to mind her confinement, and when a spirited group of Swedes in the common room next to her tiny cage began demonstrating skiing techniques by shooshing off chairs and into each other, her voice boomed over theirs: 'Keep your bloody feet off the furniture!'

Snatching the coins from my palm, she said, 'You want a key?'

'To the room?' I asked.

'Yep.'

'Well, yeah,' I said. I had assumed such a thing would go without saying.

'It's another pound fifty, luv.'

It was then that I realised that calling the London Quest a hotel was fairly optimistic on the part of the owners, but I was not to be daunted. The price, after all, was right. So I dragged my pack across the grimy carpeting to my room on the first of six floors. It was jammed full with eight steel cots piled in twos like berths in a ship, its manila-yellow walls blank but for the numerous scuff marks from the cots' steel frames. A double lancet window with stained-glass panes had been cut into the far wall, giving the room an illusion of height. At the foot of each cot were a folded pump-kin-coloured blanket, flat sheet, deflated pillow encased in stiff white cotton, and a list of shower room rules. I was later informed by Annie, the voluptuous manager, that the shower was available for only two hours each day. 'So no lally-gaggin', eh?' she warned, the wattle of her tricep wagging with her finger.

The aisle between the cots was just wide enough to walk through, but various backpacks, their colourful contents spilling out, jutted from beneath the beds, obstructing even this small path. After tripping several times, I hoisted my own pack onto one of the top bunks, thankful that without a bureau or ward-robe, there was no need to unpack.

Thus relieved of my burden, I began to investigate the putrid but oddly familiar odour that hung in the small room, aware that

I may not have shed my antiseptic Americanism as thoroughly as I had imagined. Though I was reputed to have the strongest sniffer in my family of eight, I couldn't identify the stench. It was certainly something familiar, but it had none of the pleasant tones associated with horse manure or rotting fruit. Rather, it was chemical and reminded me of the tanning factory near my home in Milwaukee but there was something more human about this smell, something sinister. No matter its origin, the stink was pervasive. As pungent right in front of the window's small slats as away, it did not seem to emanate from any particular source.

This fetid scent would plague me throughout the duration of my stay at the Quest. It infiltrated my dreams to the point where I spent my unconscious hours wandering through dirty locker rooms, dripping sewers and skunk-infested woods. After a time, I became certain it had permeated all of my clothing, my hair and even my skin. I blamed it for the lethargy into which I would fall for the three months of my stay. For now, though, I didn't worry; I merely angled the window slats to allow more air flow, and went out for coffee.

The Quest served only breakfast – a hard roll, jam and coffee – but I found there was a small kitchen where guests could cook other meals, and a tiny refrigerator for storing food, although it was doubtful that anything left one day would be there the next. The dining room had a television and VCR on which there was always playing one of the five movies Annie checked out to the guests. Tonight, and every night for the next week, *Dog Day Afternoon* ran four times in a row. Lodgers watched with varying degrees of interest, directly proportional to the length of their stay thus far. Occasionally, those who had been forced to endure the film for months on end would chant along with Pacino: 'at-ti-ca! at-ti-ca!' Sometimes two or three people would take parts and act out the scenes to perfection. Those less interested smoked cigarettes while talking of home and playing backgammon, reading old magazines or planning their next trips.

It seemed that the kids from 'Down Under' were expected to travel the way American kids were expected to go to college: the longer they stayed away, the more prestige they gained with their mates back home. Because the airfare was so expensive from Australia and New Zealand, and because as members of the Commonwealth they could work legally, London became a rest and work stop between journeys. They worked hard at lousy jobs – waitressing, nannying, construction or on factory lines – and they drank even harder. They also fucked often and indiscreetly, as I was to quickly discover.

Exhausted from my journey, I retired to my bunk after the second run of *Dog Day*. The stench hit me violently as I opened the door to my room. It smelled of decaying bodies, flatulence, sweat socks and things my olfactory glands could not even place. After a final whiff of fresh air, I flashed the lights on – then off again when I saw that people were already asleep in the beds. Under the light of a streetlamp, tinged blue by the stained glass, I pulled off my jeans and T-shirt, too tired to care that some of my sleeping roommates were male. Annie hadn't mentioned anything about the rooms being co-ed, but by this point it seemed only a minor detail. Pulling on a clean shirt, I made my bed in a rudimentary fashion while trying not to step on the knees and elbows of the unconscious man in the bunk below mine. With my hands shielding my nostrils, I fell quickly asleep.

If I had been brought up in California, I would have thought it was an earthquake that jarred me awake. Milwaukee had only the duel-pistoned Ladish Hammer which forged steel and shook the ground throughout the night. When I was awakened by the jiggling of my bed, I assumed the third-shift factory workers had thrown the hammer's switch. One sniff of the rancid air brought the reality of my location back to me, and the moans issuing from beneath my bunk made the source of the quakes all too clear.

The absurdity of other people's sex is impossible to ignore when one is perched above them in the dark, unwillingly along for the ride. At first I was embarrassed, as though I had walked in on someone in the bathroom. I tried not to move. The rhythm quickened, the breaths became breathier, and skin slapped against skin. I couldn't help picturing cartoon fish flopping on dry land, and stifled an adolescent giggle, remembering childhood laughing fits during Mass. Attempting to resist my urge to laugh, I tried to imagine who was 'down under.' Surely it wasn't the scared-looking blonde who had seemed so scandalised by Pacino's would-be transsexual lover. Perhaps it was the lusty woman who sucked sour balls as she played checkers? I couldn't stand the mystery any longer and leaned over the edge of my cot to peek. In the light of the streetlamp I saw it: like a medal of honour, '100% Grade A' was tattooed onto the skin of Annie's fleshy, flopping buttocks.

For the three months I shared the charms of the London Quest, I would drink more beer, smoke more hash and sip more coffee than is healthy, even for the young. I would learn of the malleability of time, which can stretch a minute into a mile's length and compress a month into the space of a single bed. I would learn to sleep late and eat often, to snooze through the sounds of sex and to tolerate the bodies of strangers. I would move from bad to worse, into a squat in the centre of Camden Town. And though I would never know the source of the Quest's pungency, within its walls I would, like Tennyson's *Lotos Eaters,* learn, live and lie reclined.

EVERYTHING COME ROUND

JAMES D HOUSTON

James D Houston is the author of eight novels, including *Snow Mountain Passage,* named as one of The Year's Best Books by the *Los Angeles Times* and the *Washington Post,* and most recently, *Bird of Another Heaven.* Among his several nonfiction works are *In The Ring of Fire: A Pacific Basin Journey* and *Farewell to Manzanar,* co-authored with his wife Jeanne Wakatsuki Houston, the story of her family's experience during and after the World War II internment. Formerly a Distinguished Visiting Writer at the University of Hawaii, and the recipient of two American Book Awards, he lived in Santa Cruz, California.

'THE BIG ISLAND is the biggest of them all,' he said, when I called from Honolulu. 'It is the youngest and also the wildest.' With an odd note of glee he added, 'Where we are, you can't even get fire insurance. Trucks literally won't come down here, the roads are so overgrown. So get your butt into Hilo by midafternoon. You don't want to be looking for this place in the dark.'

I'd recently landed a short-term job at the University of Hawaii and had flown in a month before teaching started, giving myself some time to roam around the islands a bit, with no fixed agenda, just to see what I could see. This back-to-the-land friend of mine from Marin County had bought a lot down on the south coast where he was building a house in an impenetrable guava and hau tree thicket. He'd put me up, he said, and be my local guide. From there I planned to island-hop back to Oahu by way of Maui and Molokai.

The day before I took off I came across an ad in the Honolulu paper for an apartment that sounded exactly like what I'd need when I returned. The only time the owner could show it to me was perilously close to my flight time, but I agreed to meet him, and that was my first mistake.

His building turned out to be almost as inaccessible as my friend's Big Island hide-out. Inaccessible to me, at any rate, still new to the city's maze of one-way streets and no-turn lanes and roads that circle old volcanic craters. I was late for the appointment, which put me out on the airport freeway during the first crunch of the afternoon commute, which caused me to miss my plane.

Sitting very still in the departure lounge, trying to quell my road rage, I told myself that landing at five o'clock instead of three was not the end of the world. If everything else went okay, I still had plenty of time to heed my friend's warning.

But everything else did not go okay. While the flight south was smooth enough, thunderheads were waiting for us in the distance. Skirting the Big Island's windward side, we dropped down through dense cloud and landed in blinding rain, the kind of downpour Hilo is famous for. My rental car was ready. The roads were not. You couldn't see five metres in front of you. I'd never known that kind of rain. I should have pulled over and waited a while. I kept thinking it would let up. How could there be enough water in the heavens to sustain this kind of deluge for more than 10 minutes? What's more, I thought I knew where I was going, having flown into Hilo once before, years earlier, on a day when the skies were clear.

I must have been half an hour from the airport when I realised I'd taken a wrong turn, maybe two wrong turns. I was lost again, disoriented this time, and running out of patience with myself. As the rains at last began to subside, a parting in the clouds sent down a dome of muted light that fell upon a cluster of shops at the end of a low-slung town. All but one of the shops looked closed, perhaps abandoned. At a corner of the parking lot stood a phone booth. I pulled in close and jumped out, taking a moment to study the sky. In the tropics, night comes early, and in this kind of weather, things could shut down fast. But I can't be that far away, I told myself. I still had time.

I dialled his number and heard 10 rings before I hung up. After missing the first flight, I'd called from Honolulu. Depending on the weather, he'd said, he might try to meet me 'up above', meaning where the asphalt ended. By this time that's probably where he was, waiting up above, a mile from his house.

So now what? Don't panic. That store looks open. Just walk over there and ask for directions. Yes, that's easy enough. But first you'd better lock the car.

I shoved a hand into my trousers pocket, only to discover an emptiness where the keys should have been. I checked inside the booth – on the floor, on the shelf below the phone. I tried the driver's door which, incredibly, was already locked. How could I have locked the door? At a glance I could see that all the doors were locked, all the windows were up, and there were the keys, one in the ignition switch, the other dangling like a tiny silver charm inside the claw machine at the county fair, the prize you'll never reach.

How could this happen? Was there some button I had pushed, or failed to push? It had been 10 years since I'd locked myself out of a car, and here I was – no tools, miles from the rental office, at the arse-end of some Big Island road, with the sun going down and more rain on its way. As the long day of mishaps caught up with me, I was suddenly exhausted, overwhelmed. I would have to do something – smash in a window or call the agency and wait two hours for a tow truck – but I needed a moment of calm, to restore my will. I leaned and placed my forehead against the car's roof – the cool and glossy curve – trying not to be defeated by a pattern of oversights and costly lapses I could now trace back to junior high. As I stood there contemplating the folly of my entire life, a voice from somewhere behind me spoke one word.

'Eh.'

I turned and saw a huge Polynesian fellow, Hawaiian or perhaps, from the size of him, Samoan. His dark features were etched and fierce. Black hair was drawn back into a stubby knot. His mouth arced in what seemed a permanent scowl, as he regarded me in the twilight of this otherwise empty parking lot.

I was thinking, Oh shit! This was exactly what you heard about. A rental car. An island visitor. Alone. At night. Somewhere in the back country. On the wrong road or the wrong beach. While seductive ads called Hawaii 'The Paradise of the Pacific', many locals had come to see escalating tourism as a threat and a scourge. Just the previous week, according to the Honolulu paper, a young French couple had been robbed at a remote camping site and beaten senseless with baseball bats. Was this to be my penance?

I glanced past him, wondering if there were others, though he didn't need any others. His brown arms, purpled with tattoos, were the size of my legs. His thighs were as thick as nail kegs. He outweighed me by 50 kilos, and it wasn't fat. If he came at me, I was finished. All his life he had hated white guys and now he had one at his mercy. I could try to outrun him, but where would I run to? Given my luck on this particular day, I'd probably run right into the jaws of something worse.

I had already surrendered, reaching for my wallet to offer what I had, when his warrior face opened in a large smile, amused and incongruously youthful.

'Eh, you need one coat hangah?'

'Coat hanger?' I said weakly, as if he'd asked me to approve his weapon of choice.

'For stick inside da window.'

'Oh right. Good.' Relief poured through me like rainwater. 'A coat hanger. Yes, that is just what I need.'

'Maybe I got one. Lemme go check 'em out.'

He wore zori slippers, baggy shorts and a vast blue-and-white aloha shirt, and moved like a sumo wrestler, arms pushed away from his body by slabs of muscle and flesh.

In my haste I hadn't noticed his car, parked in the shadows near a leafy and neglected hedge – a long-hooded Ford Fairlane once painted green, so riddled with rust holes large and small you might think someone had used it for target practice.

Opening the trunk he rummaged through a clutter of automotive debris and emerged with a wire coat hanger. As he lumbered toward me his thick hands straightened it.

'Found 'em,' he said.

'You're saving my life.'

'No big thing.'

After shaping a tiny hook at one end, he selected a window that was not shut tight and forced the wire over the top edge. Once it was inside he wriggled it back and forth, fashioning curves and angles as it descended, until he had the hook around the little tube that clicks up and down to lock and unlock the door. He moved with such speed and dexterity it was clear he had wide experience in the techniques of liberating vehicles. I gave a prayer of thanks that he hadn't come upon my car parked somewhere out by itself and unattended. I watched his nimble fingers tug and lift until the latch clicked.

With an ironic grin he handed me the wire. 'You wanna keep this? Just in case?'

'Maybe I should hang onto it. I still don't know how this happened.'

'Where you going anyhow?'

I told him the name of the road I'd been searching for.

'Right on my way,' he said. 'You like follow me?'

Under darkening skies his heavy features, for an instant, seemed menacing again. Anxiety came rising up, a lingering flicker of paranoia, as it occurred to me that this might not be a rescue after all, but some ploy to lure me out of the parking lot and further down a road of no return.

I almost said no, I could find it on my own. But that boyish smile lit up his face – a welcoming smile is what it was, a forgiving smile – and then I wanted to hug him. Maybe I should have. I thanked him again, told him I'd buy him a beer.

Nodding in a way that did not mean yes and did not mean no, he said, 'Hey, one time maybe I get stuck, you come by, do da same. Everything come round, you know.'

He bunched his thick brow with a glance into the dusk and spoke as if prompted by something unseen, over there at the edge of darkness.

'Dey call it da Big Island. But it's not that big. Everything come round and round and round.'

Easing into the Fairlane, he had to sit down sideways, then turn and squeeze his immense frame behind the steering wheel. The engine roared to life and I followed him out of the parking lot, into the wild and sultry night.

A SLIGHT LEANING BACKWARD

GREG TULEJA

Greg Tuleja was born in New Jersey and received degrees in biology and music from Rutgers University. He has worked as a professional musician, piano technician and flute teacher. Greg is currently the Academic Dean at the Williston Northampton School in Easthampton, Massachusetts, where he also teaches 9th grade English and coaches the girls cross-country team. His poems and short stories have appeared in various literary journals and magazines, including the *Maryland Review, Romantics Quarterly, Thema* and the *Journal of the California Literary Society*.

IN 1974, WHEN I WAS 23, it was not uncommon for a young person to gather together a few dollars, strap on a backpack and spend part of a summer hitchhiking through Europe, searching for unknown foreign adventures or merely trying to postpone the inevitable adult responsibility called 'work'. Europe was cheaper and safer then, and for many of us who had just finished college, it seemed to beckon irresistibly from across the Atlantic, a powerful magnet to hungry seekers of romance or naïve pretenders to what is considered cultural enlightenment.

Though I shared some of this inspiration for European travel, I also had something else in mind, something that gave my first trip to Europe a unique quality. Unlike my more practical fellow travellers who had scraped together modest but sufficient funds for their journeys, I had not saved enough money to last the month I hoped to stay in France. But I had a plan that I thought would set my trip apart from the rest – I would earn my own way by playing flute in the Paris metro.

Arriving in Paris with a great deal of formal instruction in flute but almost no training in French, I settled into one of several student hotels that lined the rue Sommerard in the Latin Quarter. It boasted a one-star classification, but I soon became convinced that absolutely no aspect of the Hotel Thillois deserved even the smallest fraction of a star. My tiny room was dark and dismally furnished, with dingy, threadbare bedcovers, no windows and an especially unfortunate feature – the closest bathroom was one floor up, and the key to that bathroom was two floors *down*.

Yet I was oblivious to this and all other inconveniences – I was in Paris and, to me, that was all that mattered. In that month I discovered that, with a little bit of effort, the necessary adjustments to a new culture could be made quite comfortably. The trip turned out to be a great success: my French improved dramatically, I played flute in the Paris metro for money, and I made a friend.

I had brought a music stand from New York and as much sheet music as I could cram into a large leather bag, and on my second day in the city, I set up for business in a bright corner of the Odéon metro station. As I had envisioned in countless dreams, I positioned myself proudly near the end of the platform and began to play the first notes. The sound of my flute filled the station, and as I played one piece after another, silver coins and the occasional paper note were tossed into my opened case by hurrying French commuters or tourists from Germany or Japan. In addition to the money, I was occasionally rewarded with enthusiastic applause; a thrilling sound that, to my ears, blended beautifully with the screeching of trains entering and leaving the station.

I played for an hour and a half each morning and afternoon, and made 30 or 40 francs a day. I was very happy.

Packing up my gear at the end of my fourth day in Paris, I was approached by a neatly dressed young man.

'Hello, my name is Henri Latelle. You play beautifully,' he said in English. 'Are you an American?'

'*Oui*,' I answered stupidly. 'I mean, yes, I am.'

'I play flute down here too, over at St-Michel. I think we could make very much money playing duos. All tips divided equally, of course. We could split everything…how do you say…fifty-fifty?'

'Yes, that's right. Fifty-fifty. Down the middle.'

'Down the middle. Yes. Well, what do you say?'

'Well, sure,' I told him. 'Do you have sheet music? All I brought with me are solo pieces.'

'I have plenty of music. I will meet you here tomorrow morning.'

'Okay. I've been starting at about 10.'

'Oh, yes, I know. I have been listening. I will see you tomorrow.'

So began a glorious month of playing music with Henri Latelle. He had a large collection of duets, familiar pieces by Telemann and Kuhlau, and also some French music I had never played – Hotteterre, Naudot, Couperin. Henri's pure joy for making music was infectious, and we performed at first mainly for ourselves, but later for ever-growing crowds of people. We gradually became celebrated fixtures in the Odéon station and made good money, which we usually squandered on food and drink, sometimes accompanied by Henri's fiancée, the elegant, inscrutable Julie.

Henri and Julie had almost reached the distant age of 30, and to me they seemed terribly sophisticated and experienced. They became my generous, warm-hearted guides to the infinite possibilities that Paris has to offer the first-time visitor. Gracious in their tolerance of my poor French, they were tireless in their efforts to introduce me to the richness and variety of Parisian life. Henri also insisted on paying for every meal, museum or concert. My polite protests to his exasperating generosity became routine.

'At least let me pay for the wine, Henri. Or the tip. Just the tip!'

'*Absolument non,* my friend, you are our guest, and that is final. And besides, here in France we have *service compris,* as you well know. There are no tips.'

'He won't listen,' said Julie. 'You might as well humour him. He always gets his way.'

Just for a moment, I noticed Henri glare at Julie. It was the first and only break in equanimity that he revealed during my entire stay in Paris: one crack in a charming facade of repose and good will. Even then Henri seemed to recover immediately, his angry expression fading so suddenly that I remember wondering if I had actually seen it at all. I am sure that I missed other clues – his occasional absences from our morning meetings at Odéon; his odd habit of wearing many layers of clothing, even in the heat of midsummer – and never did I question the yellow pill that Julie offered to him every day, precisely at noon. I was too busy enjoying myself to pay much attention to the suggestion that anything could be wrong.

After a month, summer ended and the time came for me to return to school in New York. We marked the occasion with a sumptuous, three-hour dinner in a small cafe on the rue des Écoles, elaborately financed by Henri. Laughing about my frequent mistakes with French grammar, we recalled some of our favourite moments, like watching sunsets from the steps of Sacré

Cœur and sailing toy boats at the Luxembourg Gardens. During that last dinner, it occurred to me that in over a month in Paris, I had seen the Eiffel Tower only occasionally from great distances and had never really gotten a good look at the Arc de Triomphe.

'That's all right,' said Julie. 'I have heard that New Yorkers spend their whole lives in Manhattan and never go to the top of the Empire State Building.'

'And it will give you a reason to come back,' said Henri.

I vowed to do that and Henri promised to visit me in the States. 'We will play on the steps of Saint Patrick's Cathedral,' he said. 'We'll make a murder.'

'A *killing*, Henri. We'll make a killing.'

'Yes, and then spend it all on a huge dinner in the most expensive restaurant we can find. Big American steaks from Texas. In America, you can pay all the bills.'

Close to tears, we exchanged addresses on the rue des Écoles and said goodbye. I flew home the next day.

About a month later, I sent Henri and Julie a long letter thanking them for their warmth and hospitality, which completely obliterated for me the stereotype of the distant and skeptical Parisian, full of scorn and suspicion towards all Americans.

A few weeks later, Julie replied. It was a short letter, in French, which I laboriously translated with the help of a dictionary.

It is my sad duty to tell you that Henri died last week. I was not present, but there were many witnesses, and the police explained to me what happened. Henri was playing flute in Odéon. Suddenly he stopped, walked to the edge of the platform and turned around. As a train pulled into the station, Henri just leaned backward slightly. It was a small movement, they said, hardly noticeable. A gentle leaning backward, that was all.

When you were here with us in Paris, I am sure you could see that I was very much in love with Henri. But I should also admit that I was sometimes quite afraid of him. Henri was so unsettled, so unpredictable. But he had a very restful summer – I think one of the best since I had known him. Meeting you was good for him and after you returned home he spoke of you often, always with fondness. But you were here for only a short time. You did not see Henri's other side. In many ways, he was unhappy. Always a little unhappy.

I thought of Henri's wish to visit New York, and that day, out of some uncertain sense of respect and longing for him, I carried my flute to Saint Patrick's. For a moment I stood there on the sidewalk, case in hand, but my intended musical gesture somehow did not seem to be a proper tribute, and in the end I decided not to play. I could not help but think that if we had played together here in *my* country, Henri would have been disappointed. I believe now what I did then: New York is not a place for playing music on the streets. Paris is better suited for it.

EGG CHILD
SARAH LEVIN

Sarah Levin's travels have taken her to remote villages in Alaska, the grasslands of East Africa, into the rainforests and mountains of South America, across the parched deserts of the Middle East, the lush western coast of Ireland, and several breathtaking cities in Eastern Europe. She has found herself in countless humbling situations throughout her journeys and has been honoured to befriend many genuinely kindhearted people along the way. She currently resides in Arizona and is working on writing her first book.

WHEN I WOKE UP it was still dark and I thought I was in the bowels of a ghost. My mosquito net hung loosely over the bed, white and gauzy and full of holes. I slapped a hand to my temple to crush a mosquito that had found an entrance, and slowly raked my fingernails over the row of bedbug bites on my elbow.

The equatorial heat, even at five in the morning, had settled over my limbs like moist candyfloss. I could hear the call to prayer being broadcast over loudspeakers in the mosque down the road, haunting and lovely Arabic words sounding brassy over the antiquated system. I shuffled to the bathroom in my flip-flops, sat on the toilet and put my face in my hands. Yesterday the doctor had said that my stomach lining was coming out, that I should take it easy. Today I could not take it easy.

Downstairs in the dining room, the kitchen staff were setting out a thermos of tea and bowls of sugar. Their brown faces were sleepy, quiet and smiling. One of the women came over with a mug and a piece of lemon. She touched my hair and said, You will be better. Have a good journey.

I had made this trip several times before. I was living in a wildlife refuge, monitoring the animals for parasites, and had to come into town every few days to use the veterinarian's microscope. As the crow flies it may have been 100 kilometres back to the refuge, but it would be five hours or more before I would see my tent. I took three tablets of Loperamide as I waited by the roadside for a minibus. They chugged along the road in droves, the drivers' faces looking hard and stern, the slim young boys who collected the fares slapping the side of the vans with callused hands. One slap meant a pick-up, two a drop-off. I lifted my arm and a van careened to the side of the road. The boy who opened the door was wearing a New York Yankees baseball cap. He grinned at me with brown-stained teeth and yammered in Swahili, and all I could catch was 'white lady'.

Pulling my scarf tightly around my head, I worked my way into the van. There was no room to sit, so I hunched over and grabbed onto the back of a seat, accidentally yanking on a young girl's hair as we rolled over a pothole. She turned and smiled gently, took the bag I was holding and nestled it in her kilt-clad lap as we braced ourselves for the next lurch.

The bus station was teeming with merchants selling bottles of orange-pink juice, rows of biscuits, tired battery-powered stereos and used T-shirts. Ticket-sellers crowded around me, yelping East African destinations in rapid succession: 'Nairobi!' 'Tanga!' 'Dar es Salaam!' Buses groaned into motion, spewing brown gobs of exhaust; men ran after them, hitting the sides, leaping into the doorways as they took off down the narrow streets. I muscled myself into a minibus bound for Moshi and looked into the horde of dark faces that had almost simultaneously turned to stare at the white girl. A pain seized my stomach and I breathlessly slipped between two elderly women, willing the Loperamide to soothe my intestines.

The bus grew more crowded. A toddler was deposited on my lap, my shoulders squeezed between the two soft women beside me. They spoke to me in slow, easy Swahili, asking where I was from and where I was going. They touched their hands to mine, and we swayed together on the long road.

The women waved, imitating my gesture, when I got off at the stand in the town of Boma ya Ngombe. The merchants again surrounded me, more desperate this time, because there were never white faces here. I shook my head slowly, over and over, glancing through their bony forms for the next bus. The wait here was never longer than five minutes, though the ride was more cramped. I was pulled on, prodded towards the window across from a man holding a chicken by the legs. The bird squawked, its eyes beady, its white feathers brushing my fingertips in a frenzied escape attempt.

It was past noon; sunlight poured through the glass like untouchable fire. I wiped the sweat from my eyebrows. My teeth chattered. The man across from me watched with bloodshot eyes, his chicken trembling on his knees.

At Sanya Juu I crawled over seven laps, the plastic bags tied

to my wrists trailing behind me. The sun had disappeared by
now, its yellow beams shrouded in clouds. I dodged a puddle and
headed toward a small kiosk by the side of the road. I asked to
use a bathroom; the woman pointed behind me to a guesthouse.
Crossing the road, I was met with the upturned glances of children, their dusty bellies poking out beneath too-small shirts. One
boy took my hand as I crossed. His feet were bare, as wrinkled
as a 40-year-old's. His hand was moist in the heat and warmed
my own.

The men outside the guesthouse dropped their voices as I
approached. I was shaking so badly that the bags on my wrists
were rustling and the men looked up expectantly. I greeted them
with a bowed head. A woman carrying a large bucket of laundry
on her head took my hand and showed me down a narrow corridor to the bathroom, a dark closet with a hole 30 centimetres
in diameter leading into a deep pit of excrement. I could hear the
rats. The men and women outside could hear me. They could
hear the sickness they all had endured so many times before rushing into that pit, and they had a bottle of warm soda waiting for
me when I finished. I could barely manage to thank them, my
face so burned with feverish shame.

The pick-up truck was laden with bags of maize and cabbage
and four other passengers. I tiptoed gingerly around them and
perched myself in a corner on top of a burlap sack. I tightened my
scarf over my head to shield from the wind, which was blowing
westward from Mount Kilimanjaro. On a clear day I would have
been able to see the long, white expanse of the summit casting
its shadow on the montane forest of the lower slopes, but today
those slopes were whisked away into the clouds and everything
was the same dull grey. The truck's engine and I shuddered in
unison as we prepared to leave.

But we weren't leaving. We moved three metres forward and
stopped while two more passengers, maybe brothers, hoisted
themselves into the pile of vegetables. They had long scars
careening across both cheekbones and were carrying handfuls of

oranges. They did not speak to anyone or look at anyone, just stared down at the stagnant pools of water in the road.

The rain started, tiny flecks of rain that seemed to boil and freeze at the same time on my skin. I opened one of my plastic bags and emptied the contents – two T-shirts and my toothbrush – onto my skirt and placed the bag over my head. The other riders watched curiously. The boys with the scars smiled stained-tooth smiles, sympathetic, amused.

After the driver had poured a jug of petrol into the tank he jogged toward one of the kiosks by the road and then disappeared. I glanced at my watch; it was getting late. In the sky I could see a stretch of sunlight between the dripping clouds, mustard-coloured instead of the white gold that had streamed down in arcs earlier.

Several minutes later the driver emerged from the kiosk and settled into the truck, revving the engine. The road, though full of potholes, resembled concrete and inspired the driver, who zipped across it and made sudden shifts in direction to avoid larger ditches. The concrete soon ended and dark, packed dirt stretched ahead, sandwiched between endless green-and-yellow fields. I focussed my eyes on a bag of maize and bit my tongue. I held my face up to the rain to cool my skin. The taller boy holding oranges asked if I was sick.

Just a little, I said.

White people are always sick, he said. I think you must be fragile, an egg child.

The village of Ngara Nairobi came into view 45 minutes later; we slowed for a herd of cattle and sheep crossing the road. The villagers followed the vehicle with their eyes and the children ran after us, shrieking greetings.

I slid off the back of the truck, pushing the damp sleeves of my sweater to my elbows. As soon as my feet touched the ground they sank deep into mud. It was sticky and cold, and moulded to my skin. As I pulled, straining my calves, my flip-flops slipped off. I stood on a drier patch of the road, looking at the bright red rubber half-buried in the mud and felt a stone in my throat. I awkwardly brought my skirt to my knees and bent down, reaching toward the mess, when the brothers with the oranges stepped beside me. The taller one yanked on the shoes and held them out to me.

For the egg child, he said. And have this, for your journey.

He handed me an orange and took his brother's hand as they walked away.

It would be a walk of nearly two hours back to my camp, and the sun was quickly dropping towards the horizon behind the clouds. There was no latrine here so I went behind a tree and due to a lack of tissues used leaves instead. I slipped all of my extra clothes on, but my sweater was still damp and the chills would not subside.

The village disappeared behind me. Far to the horizon I could see only trees and long stretches of savannah. I walked by several tilting houses with tin roofs, chickens in the yards, bare-bottomed toddlers. The hem of my skirt faded from white into dusky brown and finally black; the women passing by had no mud on their clothes and looked as though they had just awoken from a refreshing sleep. Even their feet appeared to glide over the mud. They seemed to wonder about me, this slovenly, pale figure.

I would not make it before dark. I hadn't brought a flashlight. I wondered what I would do and then I vomited into the bushes.

As I stood and watched the sky darkening, I heard the rusty wheels of a bicycle come to a halt behind me. The boy was my age, it seemed, and skin and bones. He asked where I had come from and where I was going. I wiped my mouth and motioned to a distant cluster of Jacaranda trees with a frantic hand.

It is too far a walk, he said. I will take you there.

He took the bags from my wrists. As he knotted them over the handlebars, I could see the tendons on his forearms and a glistening in his face. His shirt was tattered and one of his flip-flops had a broken strap. He was still for a moment, looking at the sky as

169

rain started to fall again, and then held his arm out to help me climb onto the bumper.

As I teetered on the back of his bicycle, the boy pedalled on, breathing hard with the extra weight. I grabbed hold of the seat with one hand and steadied myself with my other hand on his back. His vertebrae felt like stepping stones.

INTO THE DARKNESS

CHRIS COLIN

Chris Colin is a former Salon.com editor, and the author of *What Really Happened to the Class of '93*. He lives in San Francisco, where he writes for the *New York Times*, *Mother Jones*, *Smithsonian* and other publications, and is the On the Job columnist for SFGate .com. He belongs to the Writers' Grotto, a collective of Bay Area writers.

I WAS PEERING out the grimy couchette window at the moon-less German forest when I thought of a hole. The hole belonged to a story told by my great-grandmother, an honest woman who died recently at nearly 100. She'd written down much about her child-hood on Western ranchland, and this particular story had stayed with me since my own. It was not a sweet great-grandmother story but a terrifying nightmare of an account:

A hole had been discovered out there on the stark, red earth of Colorado; a crowd gathered when a local man agreed to be lowered. This was murky territory, where hopeful new towns built schools and markets, but also where Indians had slaughtered and been slaughtered. At first they lowered him slowly, I imagine, then a little faster as they realised just how deep a thing they were dealing with. Down he went. It's the darkness that I imagined as a boy, levels unknown to me but somehow known, too, deep in my heart. Further and further he went until finally there was too much quiet for anyone to feel good about. The others looked at each other and reeled him in. The man who finally surfaced was not the one who'd descended. Ghosts? Dead bodies? His own unravelling? Here the account was deliciously unsatisfying: what happened in that hole would remain a mystery because the man never spoke another word for the rest of his life. He'd lost himself.

A grown man myself now, I still dread and long for such a fate in embarrassingly equal proportions. One feels similarly divided on the Golden Gate Bridge, on the deck of a ship: Oh please don't let me sail over the edge... But I wonder what it's like to sail over the edge? I'd bet an Indian penny Columbus half-believed the earth was flat and that an awful plunge lay ahead. Who isn't drawn to uncertain places? For every lighthouse we build, its inverse hovers in the periphery – a pinprick of darkness beckon-ing us from the dull safety of a clear, sunny day.

But I wasn't beckoned, not really. Instead I built a life of lightness. Via busyness and easy California fun, my wife and I strayed far from that hole; the Colorado story became a funny old anecdote. So six months ago Amy and I looked at each other and decided to let out the line.

We were flip at first. We staggered around Amsterdam's Schiphol airport, exotically bright, tickets in our fists. We had seven months ahead, multiple cities, a gradual descent into the small Balkan city of our disrupted new lives and so, we thought, a descent into darkness itself. We'd quit jobs, rented out the house, even purchased coats – technological things, feats of fabric mastery – to better facilitate the descent. We laughed in different accents, moved the savings into checking. 'Are we being too cavalier?' I'd asked a good friend the drizzly afternoon we moved our belongings into long-term storage. We were leaving him and others and all family behind. But my question rang hollow and my friend and I both knew it. I was already gone.

We miscalculated the exchange rate that first day, lived briefly as kings: a beer at lunch, the finer species of postcard. We walked and rented bikes and listened to conversations in the rain. When the wind came up the Prinsengracht I felt pleasingly fortified in my new coat, as the castle guards must have when the mongrels were coming and the hot oil had been readied. The homes were wonderfully squished and the cars, too, more like a drawing of a car; cosily they puttered past on the little brick roads. Life in Amsterdam seemed as cheerful and clear as a Richard Scarry picture book – this man's climbing a ladder for the phone company, that one's delivering bread!

And so we moved along. Cheerful and clear are fine but not for getting lost. We wanted uncertainty, risk, confusion of the self. To the vast Central Station in the heart of town we dragged our suitcases and boarded the 12-hour night train to Prague via Frankfurt.

This is where I found myself in the dirty couchette, staring out at moonless woods and the occasional creepy village nestled therein. Werewolves live there. Lonely patches of dirty blue snow live there. The trees thicken impossibly, darken impossibly. We told each other ghost stories. They were the cheesy kind, leaning too heavily on bad spooky voices, but we shuddered dutifully. On a slow curve I fixed my eye on a lonesome cottage far into the trees and shadows. Were the train to stop and an official-looking person to order us off – there in the pitch-black, no choice but to rap on a yellowed window – the heart would crack apart from fright and solitude. This is *nowhere*, I thought.

But I was kidding myself. Depressingly the fantasy fell away and I conceded this wasn't nowhere – it was Germany. Sure, the terrain was peculiar and the trees a different variety, but the strange souls who inhabit these fairy-tale spots, well, they still get the zipper stuck on their coats, still shake their heads at the to-do list on the fridge. In this I, myself, was still recognisable, was not lost. The train shuddered through more woods but I put my head down. At 3.30, when the border police rapped urgently on the door of our couchette, danger vaguely suggested itself again. Grimly they searched my backpack – perhaps they'd find that half-smoked joint from Amsterdam? – but it was a superficial search. They smiled and stamped our passports and moved on to the next door with a stern nod.

Four days in Prague, four in Vienna. At the giant Disney castles and the Ringstrasse of Habsburg extravagances, we futzed with the camera; meanwhile I squinted around for the eerie sublime, for passage to the unknown and terrifying. I found souvenir crystal shops. I also found deeper things – at the architecturally miraculous Hundertwasserhaus I recalled that the sublime lurks in joy as well as in mysterious holes – but mainly I put my eggs in the dark Balkan basket looming ahead.

Down we went. Some dirty patches of snow, pale sky like a dishrag and at last our train crossed the Slovenian border. Studies in loneliness dotted the countryside: a windswept bus stop on a deserted highway, an old woman shuffling along a gravel path, a single sooty European bulldozer moving bleakly over some carcinogen mound. Meanwhile streams and rivers meandered in unholy sour-apple green.

We squealed into Ljubljana. Our friend met us and we drove

to his concrete, Socialist-era apartment; we'd stay there until we could rent one of our own. '*Dober dan,*' we said to Slovenes we saw. It was a promisingly dark greeting.

'It is a quiet building,' the agent told us in broken English, five days after our arrival. 'Many ladies.'

With that we accepted the key to our Slovenian apartment, an unexpectedly modern and luxurious building: how did this country find out about recessed lighting, we thought, and what's with all the settings on the oven?

I quickly realised I'd been wrong about everything. I knew better but still I'd expected a bombed-out capital, a crater. Instead Ljubljana was tidy and lovely, untouched by the madness that engulfed neighbouring countries just 15 years ago. Along the narrow river dividing the small city, locals sipped coffee and discussed philosophy. Or at least I imagined they were discussing philosophy. They'd grin and reach in the air for ideas, buy second rounds of grog. All around, sparkly lights pulled warm yellows and oranges from the old buildings. Sure, Ljubljana's castle floated ominously on the hill over town. But it was a pleasant kind of ominous, and I heard the cafe at the top had good coffee. In the Balkans, Bram Stoker wrote in *Dracula,* 'every known superstition in the world is gathered.' But he hadn't been to Slovenia.

And so we began a life. If I was disappointed at all the swellness – it was swellness I'd wanted a break from, back in cushy California – I chided myself for my foolishness. Anyway, there were linens to buy, spatulas to buy... Our first night in the apartment we spread a makeshift tablecloth and cooked lentils.

I didn't see it coming. Nobody sees things coming when they're chewing lentils. But it hit me harder than any haunted German forest, any imagined Balkan pandemonium. I put my spoon down.

Where am I?

The weight of our gallivanting came to me. In an impulsive moment we'd cut friends, family, television, internet, magazine subscriptions and every other diversion from our lives; all that remained were the bones. For all my interest in finding a heart of darkness on the road, I've never been good at confronting my own. In practice I prefer to glimpse the inner realm in short, sideways glances, if at all. The embarrassing truth descended on me, there at the table: I'm a flitter, a reader of the backs of cereal boxes, a phoner of pals. It didn't matter that this was happening in Slovenia, we could just as easily have picked St Louis – I was briefly, invisibly, lost.

I considered writing a postcard, beating a path back to familiar ground. But I had not come here to retreat, I told myself. I stared, and I think Amy did, too. The evening stretched before us like a desert; there is panic as well as opportunity in the unbroken, unbusy expanse of time. All that remained for us were the bones, yes, and the sight of them opened a dark, bottomless pit in the middle of that desert.

This is the essence of travel, or at least travel taken to completion: it's not the change of scenery or the new way of preparing lamb – it's *you*. You are lost to yourself, you don't know who will emerge from the pit.

After some time I cleared our bowls. A partner knows uncertainty when she sees it, but Amy said nothing. We washed the dishes and dried them, noting minor differences in Slovenian soap. The lentil bag received a knot and returned to the cupboard. We gave the kitchen a final inspection and went to the living room, where we parked ourselves on the stark white couch. We'd bought a crossword puzzle book at the airport, and it beckoned us from the floor. But we didn't open it, not this night. Instead the time somehow passed, and later we were in bed, a place both reliable and foreign when on the road, and I assume we fell asleep because we awoke the next day and it was bright.

WALKING THE MOUNT KAILASH CIRCUIT

TONY WHEELER

The *New York Times* called him 'the trailblazing patron saint of the world's backpackers and adventure travelers' and more than 30 years after he wrote the very first Lonely Planet guidebook, Tony is still regularly on the road. Walking is the one means of transport you simply cannot speed up, and the circuit of Tibet's holy mountain, following a long walk up through western Nepal to the Tibetan border, is one of the walking trips he tries to fit in each year. Tony's current travels can be found on his blog on the Lonely Planet website (www.lonelyplanet .com/tonywheeler).

BLAM! THE MAD TIBETAN slammed his head against the windscreen with such force that cracks shot across the screen from the point of impact.

Whack! He reared back and repeated the procedure. More cracks flashed out across the screen, which now bulged ominously inwards.

Wait a minute, I thought. Surely this shouldn't be happening to me. I'm sin free. When you've just wiped out the sins of a lifetime, the last thing you expect to find is a mad Tibetan trying to climb in the car with you – through the front windscreen.

It must have been 1980 when I first heard of Mount Kailash, and although I was unaware of its sin-washing potential at the time, it was instantly filed on my 'I'd like to go there' list. I'd been staying just outside Pahalgam in Kashmir, and every day hordes of Indian pilgrims had passed by on their way up to Amarnath, where each year a sacred column of ice would appear in a remote cave. It was no mere frozen stalagmite which inspired thousands of worshippers to make the tough trek north. No, the icy phallic symbol was exactly that – a manifestation of Shiva's lingam, the very penis of the Hindu faith's great creator and destroyer. Not too far from this important Shiva site was an even more significant location: Mount Kailash, the comfortable residence of Lord Shiva and his gorgeous partner Parvati. The only trouble with Shiva's mountaintop home was that it was on the wrong side of the Himalaya, north of the main range in Tibet. And back in 1980, Mao and his mates weren't exactly putting the welcome mat out.

Then things changed. China opened up a little, and a bit later Tibet as well. Soon intrepid travellers were finding their way to the furthest corners of the Tibetan Autonomous Region, as the Chinese dubbed the controversial country. There could hardly be a more remote corner of the world than Mount Kailash, tucked away in Tibet's wild west. It has always been that way. Mount Kailash has been a magnet for Hindu, Buddhist, Jain and Bönpo (followers of the ancient pre-Buddhist religion known as Bön) pilgrims for centuries, but getting there has never been easy. Today there may be no bandits waiting in ambush but there's still no simple way of approaching the holy mountain. Getting to the base of the mountain means a week's drive over lousy roads or, as we did, a similar spell on foot from the nearest mountain airstrip in the far west of Nepal.

Nor is merely getting to the foot of the mountain the end of the matter. Having arrived, you now have to walk around the mountain, to perform a *kora* if you're Buddhist, a *parikrama* if you're Hindu. The 50-kilometre circuit is a one-day sprint if you're a typically enthusiastic Tibetan Buddhist; a more leisurely three- or four-day stroll if you're a Hindu pilgrim with the odd holy lake demanding a ritual submersion along the way. The latest pilgrims, the Western ones, also opt for the three- or four-day circuit.

On a crystal-clear, sunny day in early September we set out from Darchen, the grubby little jumping-off point to the south of the mountain. We were a big group: six Westerners, a Sherpa trekking crew we'd brought up with us from Nepal and no fewer than 13 yaks to cart our tents, camping equipment and supplies. This was *kora* luxury, but it was no wonder the air was so crystal clear – there wasn't much of it. Even our starting point was at 4560 metres, and by the time we topped the Drölma La pass on the other side of the mountain we'd be at 5630 metres, up at Everest Base Camp altitude.

Only an hour into the walk we came to the *kora*'s first *chaktsal gang* or 'prostration point'. Here, pilgrims – and trekkers too, if they're determined to get into the spirit of things – sprawl flat out on the ground, hands pointed like a springboard diver towards the holy mountain. Of course, if you're a very enthusiastic Tibetan pilgrim, the first prostration point will not actually be the site for your first prostration. No, the real enthusiasts prostrate themselves for the whole 50-kilometre circuit! This does, of course, take a little longer than the usual *kora* stroll. Count on three weeks if you're contemplating making a flat-on-your-face circuit of the holy mountain.

Back on our feet we strolled on to the Tarboche, a gigantic prayer flagpole erected during the mountain's major annual festival, Saga Dawa. Tibetans may put a great deal of effort into prayer and pilgrimage, but they economise wherever possible; prayer flags are one of the most visible signs of this efficiency drive. Print a prayer or mantra on a flag and with each windy flap the prayer is carried away to the heavens. Red, white and green prayer flags can be seen strung across mountain passes and flying above monasteries right across Tibet.

Beyond the Tarboche's enormous prayer flag collection we entered the spectacular Lha Chu Valley, running along the western side of the mountain. We lunched beside the valley's swift-flowing river, made a short side trip to visit the hillside Chuku Monastery, then spent the rest of the afternoon walking north, the west or ruby face of Mount Kailash brooding above us.

There was ice on our the tent next morning and groups of Tibetan pilgrims were already striding resolutely past us along the opposite bank of the river. Swinging their prayer wheels as they marched, they had left Darchen before dawn, in order to complete their circuit in one long day. Once the sun had crept above the mountain we soon defrosted and recommenced the *kora*. We waded across the icy Dunglung Chu, cascading down from a side valley, and passed a head-high stone carved with the sacred Tibetan mantra *Om Mani Padme Hum*: 'Hail to the Jewel in the Lotus'. Late morning found us picnicking below the *kora*'s second monastery, Dira-puk.

It was only an hour's climb beyond the monastery to our second night's campsite at 5210 metres. Any higher could have presented us with problems; some of our group were already complaining of headaches, an early sign of altitude discomfort. That extra bit of height would, however, make the next day's ascent of the Drölma La an easier proposition. The north face of Mount Kailash towered directly above our campsite, only a stone's throw away, and a couple of us spent the afternoon walking up to the glacier tumbling down from the face, a short and furious snowstorm coating us white.

It was even colder the next morning, but fortunately sunlight covered us before we'd even finished breakfast, and the steady climb towards the pass soon thawed us out. There was plenty to be seen on the ascent. First we came to Shiva-tsal, where pilgrims envision their death and subsequent rebirth. Leaving an item of clothing at the site symbolises the casting off of one life and the preparation for the next, and as a result Shiva-tsal looks like a huge open-air secondhand clothes market. As we carried on uphill I glanced back at my spider underpants, draped across a rock. Maureen had always said they were a clear indication of my childish bad taste.

We soon came to Bardo Trang, the sin-testing stone. Walking around Kailash is said to wipe out all the sins of your lifetime. A serious sin cleansing, however, wiping out all the sins of *all* your lifetimes, takes a much larger commitment: a ticket to nirvana requires 108 circuits of the mountain. Nevertheless, even a minor one-lifetime scrub up is only possible if you start out with the right attitude, and a sin-testing stone checks your karma quota. The test is simple: you just have to slide through the narrow passage under the stone. Too much sin and you'll get stuck, no matter how skinny you are. And if you have too much sin, a single circuit may simply not be enough to tidy up your life. Fortunately, I slipped through without any difficulty…well, perhaps my hips were just a little wider than I expected.

From there it was climb, climb, climb until the prayer-flagged saddle of the Drölma La came into view. We relaxed in the chilly but sun-dappled air, watching a steady stream of pilgrims arrive at the pass, chanting '*Ki ki so so la gyalo,*' the traditional Tibetan pass-crossing mantra. One cheerful group of pilgrims arrived at the pass from the opposite direction, their counterclockwise circuit of the mountain confirming that they were not Buddhists but Bönpos.

Down the other side of the pass we soon came to Gouri Kund, the Lake of Compassion, where the unfortunate Hindu pilgrims are supposed to enjoy another ritual immersion, even if it requires breaking the ice before jumping in. Sensibly, the Tibetans have never held much store with this washing lark, which the Hindus are so keen on. Then it was down, down, down, traversing a lunar landscape of bare rocks and boulders, until we eventually arrived at the Lham Chu Khir, the eastern counterpart of the western side's Lha Chu Valley. Halfway through lunch it began to hail, continuing on for the next hour as we trekked south down the valley, reminding us once again that correcting a lifetime's sin doesn't come easy.

That night we camped on yet another grassy riverbank; Tibet, for all its spartan hardships, had no trouble at all in turning out a succession of idyllic campsites. The next morning we were iced in once again, but it was only a short stroll down to the final *kora* monastery, the Zutul-puk, or 'miracle cave'. Another hour's walk spilled us out of the narrowing valley on to the flat Barkha plain, from where it was just another hour or so back to our starting point, slummy Darchen.

Where our Tibetan run-in took place. Countless people were milling around in the hotel's dismal compound as we packed a truck and two Land Cruisers with our trekking gear and our Nepalese trekking crew. There were pilgrims arriving and departing, Tibetan souvenir sellers, local drivers and guides, the odd Western traveller cycling in from Kashgar, out-of-place Chinese PLA soldiers…and one increasingly drunken Tibetan. Staggering back and forth, beer bottle in hand, he'd become more and more abusive and unpleasant with each swig. He'd already had an altercation with one of our Nepalese crew, but then, just as we were driving off, he suddenly flipped out completely and flung himself at the car.

The windscreen bulged inwards once again with the third head butt, and when it showed no sign of giving way he reached under his jacket and pulled out a viciously large knife. We tumbled out of the car and scattered in all directions. For the next 20 minutes he ricocheted back and forth across the compound, far too drunk to catch anyone. Finally, like the cavalry riding in to save the day in a B-Western movie, the local PSB (Public Security Bureau) honcho turned up.

And shot him.

Not dead, just in the leg. When it heals up and he's let out of jail, it will probably take him a *kora* or two to sort out his supply of bad karma.

ON THE TRAIL
KARL TARO GREENFELD

Karl Taro Greenfeld is the author of *Speed Tribes,*
Standard Deviations, China Syndrome and the recently
published *Boy Alone: A Brother's Memoir,* about his
autistic brother Noah. He has been a writer and editor
for *The Nation, Time* and *Sports Illustrated,* was the
managing editor of the *Tokyo Journal,* the editor of
Time Asia and one of the founding editors of *Sports*
Illustrated China. His stories have been included in
Best American Travel Writing, Best American Sports
Writing, Best American Short Stories, Best American
Nonrequired Reading and *Best Creative Nonfiction*
anthologies among others.

WHEN I WAS WORKING IN CHINA, it seemed that everyone I needed to see was not where he was supposed to be. He was away, at the county seat, or at the provincial capital, or visiting relatives in a distant region. Or I couldn't find out where he was, exactly, but he certainly was not here, in this office or bureau or work unit I had travelled 1000 miles to reach. 'Here' was always past the edge of a town where stores sold nothing but tractors, motorcycles and spare parts for trucks – gleaming new manifolds, greasy axles and engine blocks, laid out in the swept dirt before a darkened showroom, beneath a red banner advertising Donfeng and First Automotive Works. Then I passed factories that seemed abandoned. And then subdivided collective farms cultivating crops I didn't recognise. And then a winding dirt road until, finally, I arrived.

And despite all my previous disappointments, the regularity with which I had failed to meet with any of those officials or politicians or civil servants I had set out to interview, my hopes would rise as I drove through the gate, past the indifferently manned guard house, to the parking lot in front of the ministry or bureau or people's hall. I remained optimistic as I climbed the three concrete steps to the unlit, dusty lobby and then waited a few moments at the reception desk. I stayed enthusiastic while the middle-aged man with the huge mug of tea, muddy with what looked like chewed tobacco, mulled my request and then shook his head because he didn't know if the official or civil servant or administrator or deputy director or under assistant or section leader or work-group subchief was in today. He would tell me where the office was – inevitably it would be on the 5th floor, and there was never an elevator. And I climbed, fulsome with aspiration, and I reached the door, stained wood with perhaps a few simple documents tacked to it outlining recent regulations and new ordinances and changes in the schedule and the announcement of a clean-up-the-city campaign and an end-littering drive, and then I knocked on the door. And I waited.

And he was not there.

And nobody knew when he would come back.

And no, under no circumstances, would they give me his mobile number.

Writing my book about the deadly new virus that would later be called SARS – tracking down through government officials the first patients afflicted by this mysterious disease – meant 100 of those trips, long voyages of hope that ended by crashing into closed office doors.

And then we would retire, my assistant and I, to a local restaurant, where we would order the local hotpot delicacy, some freshwater fish cooked with chillies, some rabbit stewed with scallions, some chicken knuckles mixed with hot peppers, and try to figure out how many *li* away was the county seat, the provincial headquarters, the big city offices. (A *li* is, technically, the distance a fully burdened imperial porter could travel in 24 hours; I don't know that anyone actually uses *li* as a measure of distance anymore, but I've always liked the sound of it and it works very well to express my exasperation at the great Chinese distances I always had to travel.) The food was always pleasantly surprising. The distances daunting. Six more hours in the back of a smoky hired car with the driver's cassette of that German song that goes 'Da da da' on autoreverse. Could he change it?

Yes, he said, but then I will fall asleep.

And so we let him play 'Da da da' all six hours, until we were at the county seat or provincial capital and then I would find out that the official, the deputy director, the workers collective boss, he was gone. And then another night in a local, even smokier hotel where I couldn't pick up a mobile phone network and the internet connection was a slow-speed dial-up that wouldn't let me read any sites that weren't in Chinese.

Is there a word for hopes that persist though we know they are certain to be dashed? It is with such totally unjustified optimism that we drive today to the village, at the end of a two-lane macadam road, past the shops selling spare truck parts and the women who have laid out a crop of some sort of red beans by the side of the road to dry in the few hours of late autumn sun. We climb the concrete steps and query the informationless reception-ist, and then ascend two more flights to the office of the deputy director of the local branch of a government agency dedicated, at least nominally, to fighting infectious disease.

We knock once and then walk into a narrow, sunny office with two tall windows facing south. On his desk is the tea mug, thick with its composting vegetative matter, an ashtray, a pack of Panda cigarettes and a plastic lamp with a calculator and paper calendar built into its base. And he is here! The sight of him, smoking his cigarettes, sipping his tea, poring over a medical-supply magazine, is as reassuring to me as finding a cheque in the mail from a maga-zine that has published a story of mine – unlikely yet still, despite everything, expected.

He is a squat man, with a short neck and a boxy, fleshy head so that if you had to render him very quickly you might start with a rectangle as his abdomen and then a smaller rectangle as the head, topped with a few quick pen strokes representing shocks of black hair combed at a 45-degree angle down and to his right. He appears well fed and has a sleepy air that could also, in a pinch, serve as a buffer to keep unwanted visitors from overstaying.

We bow. I explain myself and my project in terms that will in no way be perceived as politically controversial. This is dry, aca-demic stuff, he should understand, of interest only to scientists, doctors, public health officials – very unlikely, in other words, to ever catch the attention of government officials in Beijing. Yet I need to appeal to him, to his vanity, to any lingering preten-sions to serving the commonweal that have survived his decades in the Chinese civil service. His cooperating with me should be understood as a totally risk-free salve for whatever might still be troubling his conscience.

He listens in his somnambulant manner, once even closing his eyes for a few seconds, and then he rouses himself and offers me a cigarette. I have a fondness for Panda cigarettes – Deng Xiaoping's brand. They were traditionally available only to high Chinese officials and a tin of them openly displayed on a bureaucrat's desk used to be an unsubtle display of connectedness – *guanxi*. The cigarettes can today be purchased in some duty-free shops and from the myriad tobacconists and cognac vendors lining the corridors connecting Hong Kong and Shenzhen in the south.

Those Pandas sold in the south, however, have a stale quality absent from the cigarettes I smoke in the presence of those officials I have met. Also, those Pandas sold on the market come in flat aqua tins while the officials always have big, round, red cans. The cigarettes from these cans, somehow, taste like illicit privilege; you know anyone smoking these cigarettes is someone or knows someone.

And now, sitting in this distant office, I know someone.

He opens his flip phone and reads out a mobile phone number.

'Is this the patient?'

'No,' he shakes his head, 'this is the neighbour of the patient. Or the patient's parents, anyway. They live in a godforsaken place, a trash heap practically. It has a name like Wasteville – no, that's not it. Waste Land? Garbage Town? Trash Village?'

It sounds like that. The man I am looking for, he has no phone. Nor do his parents. It isn't even a village, where they live. Just a collection of shacks, lean-tos. These people are not even native to this place which doesn't have a proper name, only a few words denoting that it was built around things other people don't want.

'This is the person you need to talk to,' the official explains. 'I have the number of the man who owns the land where all these people make their shelters. They are dirty people. Filthy.'

'Is he there? The patient?'

The official nods in a way that means maybe, maybe not.

And I know that means another 10 hours sitting in a car, driving through the Chinese night, looking for a place and a person who I hope will be there, but who I am sure will not.

I changed assistants a month or so ago. My first was a rough woman named Hu who dressed like a boy and seemed indifferent to whether we succeeded in any of our intended visits. She walked with a rolling gait, like a cowboy, and she never carried a pen or notebook into any of our nonappointments. This shouldn't have bothered me. These were, after all, nonappointments. No one was ever there so there were no interviews so why should she have bothered to bring a pen or paper. But I felt it jinxed us, somehow, to not even maintain the pretence that our official, our deputy director, our little mandarin, might actually be here.

My luck was rotten, I concluded, so I needed to change it. And I hired this lovely little Sichuanese woman, Zhu, with pointy shoes, a narrow waist, wavy hair and big, round, brown eyes. And she was still excited enough about the idea of journalism, of working on a story, a book even, that she always carried a little dossier inside of which was a pen, a fake leather notebook and even a few extra pens.

And here she sits, leaning forward in her chair, her little notebook open before her, those big eyes beaming at this Panda-smoking official. His phone is flipped open, and Zhu asks in her sweet little voice, does he have any other phone numbers that might be helpful, other doctors, government officials, hospital directors, epidemiologists? He takes a drag on his cigarette, looks us both over, lingering for a while on Zhu's exposed calves, and then begins to read off the phone numbers he has saved in his mobile, his web of contacts and secret phone numbers.

We scribble furiously, at least two dozen phone numbers, names and titles, many of them names we have read in newspapers and World Health Organization reports. I don't know that Zhu understands what we are being given; part of her charm is that she takes for granted her access and ability to win confidence. I also try to take it in stride but I am overjoyed and can't help but feel that finally, all those journeys of 10,000 *li* have not been wasted.

We start with the very first number he has given us, the phone of the man who knows the man I want to see – the first patient, possibly the index case, the embodiment of emergence, at which the incident that I am writing about begins.

Another long drive, this one with a taxi driver who does, at one point, fall asleep for a few seconds before alert Zhu nudges him awake from her seat beside him in the front. Every 100 kilometres or so, there are huge pyramid-shaped gas stations at the side of the road, little pennants drooping from nylon cords attached to the broad eaves. Sometimes, as in the West, convenience stores are attached, with their antifreeze and cans of motor oil and packs of cigarettes and cans of Pringles. (Pringles are everywhere in China. I don't know how or why, but there they are, on sale in myriad flavours next to baskets of live grub beetles and strands of dried roots and bound coils of copper wiring.) Finally, we pull into a parking lot, rent rooms at a hotel, and I crawl into a wood-framed mattress that smells of nicotine, in a cold room with a concrete floor that has an open drain in one corner. All night, I imagine that I am hearing insects crawl from the drain into my room. In the morning, when I wake up, there is a centipede halfway out of the drain, its antennae whirling in the frigid air. Before it can finish its reconnaissance, I bring the heel of my loafer down, making a wet crunching sound much like smashing a grape.

At breakfast, the driver sits at a separate table and slurps down a bowl of rice porridge between cigarettes as I drink green tea and eat Pringles from a can.

We drive another four hours and arrive, finally, at the bottom of a foothill covered with pale trees that look, from a distance, like stunted spruce trees. At first glance, this little mountain looks pleasingly sylvan, the high ground beside a slow-moving channel of greenish water. There are numerous trails of smoke rising from what I imagine are cooking fires, the hearths of the encampments of the hardy woodsmen living in this alpine hamlet. We call the number given by the official, and the information we receive is the usual vague information cloaked in what we take to be the standard suspicious misdirection. The man may be here, members of his family certainly are, somewhere. We may find them. We may not.

Now we have to find the man who knows the man. But he, alas, is now away. At a meeting. In another town. Many *li* away.

We do learn where we might find the first patient or at least his family. They are up the hill. Zhu and I start climbing a muddy, switchback trail, and very quickly I realise how mistaken I was about the bucolic nature of this little mountain. First of all, these trees aren't stunted but have been systematically denuded of any material that might serve as fuel. What I had taken to be a ground cover of foliage is actually a form of refuse I have never encountered, the discarded, broken-up plastic shells of old computers, televisions, fax machines, high-tech waste of familiar brand names, slightly burned, muddied and trod into the ground. I have never seen this sort of trash extruded and dumped in this manner, as if birds had defecated vast amounts of plastic guano.

At the first encampment, we see that what I had assumed to be cooking fires are actually smelting pots in which bright, liquefied metals shimmer like undulating tin foil. It is beautiful. It smells lethal. We ask a withered fellow sitting on a cement block and wearing sandals made from an old tyre for the man we have come to see. He does not know him. But he knows his clan. They are further up the hill, at another encampment. And we climb some more, the plastic casing cracking underfoot. Finally, near the top, where another pot simmers a liquid that is more dull and pewterish in colour than that which cooks down the hill, we find another scavenger who has bundled himself in a drab, olive parka as he sits on a bench made from what looks like the casing of an old, orange iMac computer. He does not greet us. Not knowing where to stand, and feeling out of place in my fancy loafers, blazer and pea coat, I pause for a moment by the fire and warm my hands until I inhale some of the fumes emanating from the cauldron. The poison makes me take a quick step back.

Zhu asks the man if he knows the patient for whom we are searching.

'Yes.'

'Is he here?'

'No.'

'Will he be back?'

'I don't know.'

'Does he have a mobile phone?'

'No.'

'Oh.'

Zhu tells him who I am, what I am doing, and I suggest that we will pay something for the man's time, if and when he ever returns.

We descend the foul mountain.

Over a dinner of some sort of ground poultry cooked in a stew with cabbage, I wonder whether I will ever gather what I need to write this book from a country so impenetrable and vast, where no one is ever where they ought to be, where appointments are rarely kept and phone calls never returned, where, when I am bivouacked in lonely towns like this, there is not a soul I know besides my assistant for 1000 miles. But I have already invested months seeking and interviewing those who could be located. My ego is linked to the completion of this book in a manner that makes me embarrassed to consider abandoning it. Books, I tell myself, are more the accumulated product of overcoming these moments of doubt and insecurity than they are the star bursts of inspiration.

Also, I have already spent a good portion of the publisher's advance.

The restaurant has rough plank walls festooned with fading beer posters. There is a woman seated behind a gouged wooden desk, which has soda and beer bottles lined up along one side and an abacus in the centre. Just as we are finishing our chicken and cabbage, three men in drab grey and olive clothing enter the restaurant. They recognise Zhu and before they can sit down at another table, she very quickly rushes to them and, it seems to me, forcefully guides them to our wobbly table. Ah, these are the men from the mountain! I recall them seated before their steel pots, melting down their salvaged precious metals. In the fluorescent light, their creased faces are sharply contrasting, narrow bands of white and shadow. I hurry to the girl at her desk and gather three bottles of beer and three more glasses. Once the men have each downed a drink, I pour another round, and then another.

They are taciturn, bashful around Zhu and a foreigner, but also, as they drink, they become less reluctant to express their curiosity about why I am here, what I am doing. They remember the virus, of course, for they themselves have a close relative who has been stricken. But they are vague about where he is, this first patient, this fellow who had the virus before it even had a name. When he fell sick, one of the men explains, everyone just assumed he had caught one of the innumerable coughing diseases that burn through China in the winter.

As Zhu pours them more beer, and encourages them to order whatever they wish, they forget for stretches that I am even there. I slide my chair back to make myself less obtrusive, and look down at my pants, study my hands, fold them, wiggle my fingers. I never make eye contact with the men who are chatting eagerly with Zhu, peppering her with questions about Sichuan, about her village, about the sorts of dishes they prepare there, and then about Beijing, where she lives, and whether she misses her family and what her parents think of her living in the city. They assume she lives in a dormitory, with other women who have jobs like she has, and they say that if they were women then perhaps they would seek that sort of job, an office job, instead of tearing apart old computers, monitors, fax machines and printers and stripping their CPUs, circuit boards and disc drives of traces of aluminium, copper and gold. They are able to extract about five *jiáo* worth of metal from each CPU or circuit board, that's about a half-penny for each man. The work is dirty, and, the men worry, unhealthy. They have been told by a doctor who travelled up to see them that they are at risk of being poisoned by the fumes that rise as they burn off the precious copper and gold. It is mercury, they have been told, and it will kill them slowly. This doctor had offered to sell them medicine but the men found it too expensive.

'And whose land is this?'

'It belongs to a mining company a few hills over.'

That was where they used to work, they explain. Two of them are even entitled to minute pensions. They supplement those irregular payments with the work up the hill.

'Does it have a name, this place?'

'Jianxi Area Mine #6.'

'No, the little mountain where you work.'

'No.'

From the woman behind the desk I collect four more bottles of beer. Since we are now the last party in the restaurant, I also slip her 400 *kuài* notes, as a tip for letting us stay late. This turns out to be another stroke of luck, as she orders the kitchen to produce a dish far better than any we have eaten so far: a hotpot of some sort with at least two medium-sized fish stewing in chillies and peppercorns. I don't know where in this landlocked province they caught these fish, but their arrival signifies that this dinner has turned into a banquet of sorts. I dish out the seafood into the chipped porcelain bowls, giving the men almost all the meat. They slurp it up happily.

'If I worked in an office,' one of the men comments, 'I would always eat seafood.'

As I gaze at the men gathered around this scratched wooden table, each of their faces withered and creased and shiny from the grease and red from the beer, I feel for the first time a pang of guilt at seeking to manipulate them by sating their hunger and thirst. Why should I take advantage of their appetites? And in a larger sense, who am I to assume that I should be able to extract from this vast country, the hardship of which is embodied in the faces of these three men who ply starvation wages from high-tech waste, anything that I could then take back to America and sell to those enjoying easy lives?

'Forget it,' I tell Zhu, 'don't worry about it.'

She looks at me strangely. She points to a fellow with a crew cut removing a fishbone from his mouth with a pair of chopsticks. 'But this is him.'

That dinner in that remote province is where my luck changes. Zhu and I begin a series of interviews and meetings where instead of closed doors and absent officials and doctors and hospital chiefs always in distant cities, they are at their desk and are happy to meet with me. We are handed documents and hospital admission forms and official communiqués and, twice, top secret, internal memos. And when I return home from these trips, I begin to write down what we are discovering, to make sense of the information we have gathered. As hard as it was before, it is inversely easy now. A friend of mine, an accountant, loans me a little office in the central district of Hong Kong where I unpack my files and open my computer and begin in earnest. I can write this book, I now feel. What I am typing might actually amount to something. Oh, it is awkward and forced and full of sentences, paragraphs, entire sections that have no place in any published work, and it is unwieldy and unsound in the way that a bridge constructed from just one bank might appear. But it is slowly, accretively, emerging, on my hard drive, 10,000, 20,000, 30,000, 40,000 words. I am nearly halfway to a finished manuscript.

In the afternoon, when I am finished writing for the day, I take a walk up Pedders Street to the Foreign Correspondents Club, where I can check my email, or I cut over to Lang Kwai Fong where I can buy a coffee at Starbucks or browse in the Front Page bookstore. I love that sense of a day's work done and stored in my computer, diligently backed up on an iPod, and of just dawdling for a few minutes, watching the pedestrians, admiring the women, scanning the crowd for anyone I might know. It is a totally earned waste of time. I'm not expected anywhere for a few minutes, and I have nothing to do.

It is on an afternoon like this that Zhu calls me and tells me the most improbable news yet. A very high official, a mandarin among mandarins, has agreed to meet with me. He wants me to come to Beijing, tomorrow, to see him.

I go, of course, packing my computer and roller bag and taking the plane from Chep Lap Kok to Beijing and then a car to the St

Regis, where I sleep fitfully. In the morning, I meet with Zhu and together we go to the ministry. I am greeted by several officials, the most senior of whom is a woman with a stack of curly hair and wire-frame glasses, who gives me her card. We are led into a meeting room where there is a mural of the winding Great Wall on the southern wall and a bank of windows facing east. The seats are upholstered with white doilies laid over the chair backs so that as I sit down, I feel the bumpiness of the stiff fabric against my shoulders. Cups of tea are positioned on small, dark wood tables arranged between each chair.

The four officials sit down on chairs beneath the east-facing windows. I sit with Zhu beside me on a bank of chairs opposite the mural. Finally, the minister himself enters, makes a very slight bow in the direction of his colleagues and then comes over to where I am standing and shakes my hand, bows again and takes the seat beside me. He wears a dark blue suit, white shirt and shiny silver tie. His jowls dangle slightly over his collar, so that when he sits I can't see his neck. One of his underlings strolls over and hands him a folder which he leaves unopened on his lap.

The interview itself does not provide me with much new material – he repeats the government position that it did everything it could, that no-one could have known this was a new disease, that the cover-up was the work of misinformed local officials who have been punished, and that the circumstances that allowed for this outbreak have been altered. Yet the meeting is symbolically significant for me. I have secured access to one of the highest officials in the land. And he is here, right where he is supposed to be.

I decide to return to Hong Kong via Shenzhen, to make another visit to one of the neighbourhoods that had been among the earliest points of infection. I have come to know this area well. The collection of eight-storey tenements is a grid of dank, wet, unpaved alleys just two metres wide. There are numerous barber poles skirling red, white and blue. (The barber pole, in China, very often denotes a house of ill repute.) The hookers in skin-tight lycra pants and tube-tops grab my arm as I walk past. Because I am a foreigner, they proffer *'Amore, amore'* – Italian here, for some reason, being the language of love. There are several tiny piecework factories of three sewing machines each; the workers sleep under their machines at night. There are four fellows who can repair your shoes, and one fellow who converts old tyres into sandals. There are a half-dozen key duplicators. And no less than a dozen doctors in one-room offices – 50-square-foot shop fronts featuring, usually, a bench covered with newspapers, a cabinet full of pills, maybe a diploma on the wall and a stool on which the MD sits, smoking cigarettes. They all specialise in treating venereal diseases, besides a frightening few who practise cut-rate plastic surgery. But it would be easier to bypass the doctors and head straight for any of the half-dozen pharmacies that do a thriving business in aphrodisiacs and antibiotics. There are the pay-by-the-call phone centres, the pay-by-the-hour hotels and the pay-by-the-tablet ecstasy dealers. You can buy one of anything here: a cigarette, a nail, a phone call, an injection, a piece of paper, an envelope, a stamp, a match, a tablet, a stick of gum, a bullet, a brick, a bath, a shave, a battery, even a feel.

There are shops punched through the walls where for a *kuài*, you can pick out a DVD or VCD from a box and watch it on a monitor and listen to the audio through headphones. You take a seat in a darkened room alongside others who are killing time. I flip through the box at a VCD parlour and choose the latest *Matrix* instalment. When I pay my *kuài* and am seated in my moulded plastic chair, I find myself instead watching *Zoolander* – in Korean. I try to explain to the proprietor, a kid with spiky black hair and knock-off Oakleys, that Stiller and Ferrell in Korean are no substitute for Reeves, Moss, Fishburn and Agent Smith, but to no avail. In the end, I have to pay another *kuài* for another flip through the box. I end up watching the first 10 minutes of *Outbreak*.

I walk a few *li* through crowded streets to the border crossing at Lo Wu, past the corridors of tobacco- and brandy-sellers with their tins of Panda cigarettes, where I catch the last MTR train back to Hong Kong. I listen to a few songs on my iPod and watch as the businessmen around me replace the Chinese SIM cards in their mobile phones with Hong Kong versions.

When we come screeching to a halt in the bowels of the station, I slip off my iPod headphones and shove the music player into my briefcase, next to my computer, sling the black briefcase over my roller bag and disembark, heading up the escalator.

There is a long, cavernous hallway down the western side of the station that is open to On Wan Street and the numerous bus lanes between that and the wider avenue beyond. In the dull fluorescent light, the commuters' tan trench coats and leather jackets are shineless and muted, seemingly as fatigued as their wearers scurrying from the late trains to the taxi stand at the front of the station.

I am also tired but with a sense of wellbeing. My many trips to nowhere Chinese towns and often futile attempts to locate officials and administrators are now paying off in the book that is growing on my laptop, right here beside me. That it will all – the reporting, the writing, the fretting – somehow add up is as optimistic an outlook as I can ever have as a writer. I stop at a corner where the corridor intersects with another from Hong Chong Road to replenish my subway and railway pass at a vending machine. I set down my rollerbag beside me, leaving my briefcase perched on top, and then fumble in my pocket for my wallet. I slide the card into the ticket machine along with a red hundred-dollar note. A few other commuters walk behind me, one coming close enough so that his coat seems to brush mine.

I turn around, shoving my wallet back into my pocket.

My briefcase is gone.

My computer, my iPod – my book has been stolen.

I howl. I have never made such a sound before.

I look both ways. There are at least a dozen people walking away from me, going in any of three possible directions. I grab my rollerbag and run down one hallway towards the bus lanes, but stairways descend from this covered walkway every 20 metres. Whoever stole my briefcase could have made off in any of a dozen directions. For some reason, I keep returning to the site of the theft, as if in so doing I can turn back time.

I felt him for a second, I think. I can almost see the person, his black coat just glancing off mine, or was that my own bag that I felt being pulled away? Why hadn't I turned sooner?

The thief can have no idea of the value of its contents. He would be delighted at the US$700 in travellers cheques stashed in a zippered pocket, at the $2500 or so Hong Kong dollars in an envelope, at the Gucci sunglasses, the Palm Pilot, the iPod and, of course, the computer. He wouldn't even be aware of my book, my transcribed notes, the thousands of hours of work that digitised information represents. These are as valueless to him as the notebooks in which I have sketched images of Guanzhou and Shenzhen, as the collection of business cards I have amassed. A magnet will be swept over the computer's hard drive to erase it, the notebooks will be tossed into a waste bin.

The police station is brightly lit, with cartoon posters advising what to do if you are cheated or in a traffic accident. There is a Cantonese couple seated in plastic chairs before a white counter, speaking rapidly in Cantonese to a uniformed officer who nods once in a while and keeps attempting to draw their attention to a form he has laid out on the counter in front of him. Behind him is a plain white wall and beyond that, I imagine, is the rest of the station. I had assumed that the two officers who had responded to my complaint would have radioed ahead to let the station know that I was coming before they put me into a van to the station. But now I realise that I am just another robbery victim and will have to wait my turn to file my complaint.

Finally, the Cantonese couple rise to leave and I take a seat. I explain to the officer why I am here, what I am doing, and he asks if I would like to file a report.

'Yes.'

He asks to see some identification. I hand him my Hong Kong ID card, which he takes with him back into the station while I wait.

I am led to a small room where I am told to sit down and the officer says, 'Robbery?'

I nod. 'Yes.'

'Did you see?'

I shake my head. I shrug. 'Sort of.'

He doesn't understand me.

'Not really,' I say. 'Is there anything you can do?'

He doesn't seem to understand this either. He looks over my ID card and begins writing my name and other information on an official report.

'What taken?'

'A computer – my book,' I tell him, almost crying again, 'my book.'

'One book,' he says, carefully writing it down. 'How much?'

I shake my head. 'My book was on the computer. I'm writing a book, and this book was on the computer.'

'Com-put-er.' He carefully enunciates as he writes. 'How much cost?'

Later, I will be told by others who have dealt with the Hong Kong police that you have the option of writing the report yourself, which would have saved an hour of watching Sergeant Yiu struggle to write, '1 pom pirate adres book w/ kebored'. But after a while, I realise that these hours of dealing with the police, of laboriously transcribing what has been stolen, of explaining, over and over, that I am writing a book and that my book was on that computer, this is part of the grieving process. I recite the litany, sounding out the words to help Sergeant Yiu phonetically spell out Macintosh, travellers cheque and Tumi. I watch as he laboriously transcribes the contents of my briefcase, never once writing down the most important thing stolen.

When he is finally finished with the report, he leaves the room and returns with a photocopy of the report and a card, which has his name, the report number, case officer and the station's telephone number and Sergeant Yiu's mobile phone number. I take the card and look at it for a moment. It is what I have been given in place of thousands of miles of travel and thousands of hours of research. I slide it into my wallet.

'Do you ever catch them?' I ask. 'Do you ever recover the stolen stuff?'

He shrugs. 'Sometimes. But I have to be honest, not so much.'

I don't know why, but I didn't expect that when the police were finished taking my report they would simply show me to the door. I'm not sure what I expected, but I wasn't ready for that to be it, for my book to be gone and the actual police response to the theft to have amounted to this. But Sergeant Yiu led me to the door and out into the waiting room with the cartoon posters and then I walked out into the street, a narrow, sloping road glistening from a steady rain that had started while I had been in the station. It was four in the morning and there were no taxis in sight and I was disoriented, not even sure which direction I should walk in to find a cab.

It didn't matter really, which way I went, because I was totally lost.

I have that card Sergeant Yiu handed to me now, more than two years later. I still carry it with me in my wallet. The Report Number is 03027895. There is his name, his DPC number, whatever that is, and then a line reading DVIT 2/HH DIV, which I believe refers to the Hung Hum Division, though I could be wrong. There are the phone numbers and, at the bottom, for some reason, a fax number. There is no date on the card but I will always remember that: 18 November 2003.

On 19 December 2003, I began to rewrite my book.

LET'S GO
EMILY PERKINS

Emily Perkins was born in Christchurch, New Zealand, in 1970. Her first short story collection, *Not Her Real Name and Other Stories,* was published in 1996, followed by the novels *Leave Before You Go* (1998), *The New Girl* (2001) and *Novel About My Wife* (2008). Since 2006, Emily has hosted a book review show on NZ television; first called *The Book Show,* it became *The Good Word* in 2009. She lives in Auckland.

LET'S GO TO ROXY, we say. Let's go to FX.

I try to learn some of the language, but don't get beyond 'diky', which means thanks. Informal. Casual. Friendly. The formal way is 'dekuji vam', but it's easier not to bother with the distinction. I find myself lost, wandering up and down a block looking for the Globe Café, (I am two crucial streets away from it, but I don't know this). I stop people and ask, Do you speak English? and they shake their heads and smile. Diky, I call after them, diky, diky. Diky for nothing!

We go to Roxy, we go to FX.

Grunge, announces Hal, hit Prague like a soggy mattress.

He's right. It looks like it's here to stay, in every bar and cafe, we visit. Americans, Americans. Thousands of dollars but they dress as if they're slumming it.

We stand outside the theatres and study the black-and-white photographs. Scenes from Beckett, Anouilh, Ionesco. Seriousness. Raised fists. Absurdity. We laugh.

We come across a candles-and-flowers shrine commemorating the Velvet Revolution. There are poems which we cannot read. Some tourists wander up and stand behind us, at a deferential distance. We don't speak until they are gone. We want them to believe what we briefly believe, that this is our memorial, our pain, our revolution. They back away with the hush of the guilty. We look at each other and we laugh. Hal reads a poem out loud in nonsensical Czech phonetics and we laugh again.

We're hungover at Segafredo and I'm cross because they don't have hangover food. I order a hot chocolate without cream.

The waitress doesn't understand me.

Without cream, I say. No cream.

She looks at Hal for help. He finds me embarrassing.

No cream, I say louder. I don't want any cream with the hot chocolate.

She frowns.

Cream? I don't want any?

I mime pouring cream out of a jug. Thick, I mutter.

Her face is blank. She tells me, It does not come with cream.

I make a mental note of this, for next time.

We go to Roxy, we go to Globe, we go to FX.

Look! says Hal. Poetry readings!

We get a cab to FX for the Saturday night poetry reading. The cab driver has a more explicit collection of pornographic pictures than most. I think about what might be in his car boot. He has a high colour and when someone cuts him out at the lights I think I see specks of foam in the corner of his mouth. His moustache makes it hard to be certain. I worry about apoplexy, and how hard it would be to gain control of the car if he were to clutch at his chest and then collapse suddenly around the steering wheel, inert.

We sit in the big armchairs at the back of FX. Some very beautiful women are there. They are all Czech, which is unusual. A – that they're beautiful (no tan stockings encasing ham-like thighs, no tasselled suede pirate boots, no lurid artificial blush applied over undemure cheeks). B – that they are here in FX, which like every other place we go to is usually inhabited by young people from everywhere in the world except Eastern Europe.

Their eyebrows are plucked excruciatingly thin and without exception they have those fashionably swollen big lips. Hal says there must be a special machine in the girls' loos – press a button and a boxing glove pops out and hits you to create that perfect punched-in-the-mouth look. He mimes being hit by it, his head jerking back in a whip-lash movement. Again! I say, clapping my hands together, Again!

The beautiful women drift in and out, past our chairs, talking intently to each other in low voices. Sheets of paper – their poems! – dangle casually from their fingertips.

Czech chicks, murmurs Hal longingly.

Learn the language, I suggest. That'd be a start.

Diky, he says, morose.

Actually I think the language barrier is no bad thing. It provides a lot of scope for meaningful looks. But it does mean that what we understand by a 'poetry reading' is not what the Czechs understand by one – after much quiet and tender-sounding talk between themselves and passing around of the pieces of paper, they stand up and flowingly, waifishly, leave.

We go to Roxy, we go to Roxy.

Hal dances. I don't, won't, can't. The vodka is cheap. It works out, per plastic cup, at 90p. Or a buck and a quarter. Or $2.50. In any currency, it's a cheap shot. Ha ha. Later, we hear that there is some poisoned Polish vodka floating around the city. It was transported from Krakow in rusty vats. More than seven shots a night, the papers say, could kill a grown man. Even so, we do not die.

The receptionist at the hotel says, There is a message for you. We're excited – a message? Who could it be from? Perhaps it is from our friend Louis who is running a bagel factory somewhere outside the city. Perhaps it is news from home, except that nobody knows where we are. Maybe, I think, it could be from the German boy I gave my number to in Chapeau Rouge last night.

But – unhappy travellers! – the message is from the hotel management. We have chipped a corner off the wooden tag attached to our room key.

You have broken this, the message says, and it was new last week. You must replace it.

We are bewildered. I hand over some kroner.

Now? I ask, unsure what to do.

As you wish, the receptionist says, taking my money and giving me a receipt which she first stamps three times.

Sorry about that, we say, and we laugh.

Prague is not a good place to be vegetarian. We go to dinner and order three or four different kinds of meat, which all arrive on the same plate but cooked in different ways. It is a flesh-fest. Hal pretends to adore it but even he is unable to finish the last piece of liver. Vegetables, we say. We want vegetables. When they come they are recently thawed diced things from out of a packet: carrot, sweetcorn, peas. Vodka, we say. We want vodka.

Ha ha ha.

Apparently, there are a number of things I do which infuriate Hal. I embarrass him in cafes (the hot chocolate incident);

211

I embarrass him in bars (the German boy incident). I talk too loudly in the street and I can be 'pretentious'. Pretentious, moi? Hal's objections surprise me. We are like an old married couple. He says 'huh' too often (he claims to be unaware of this) and his jaw clicks when he eats. Or is that my father? I can't be sure.

It's too hot in our hotel! The radiators are up full blast. Gusts of warm air chase us down the halls. Our room is a little heat pit. I wake up with gunky eyes and burning sinuses.

The hotel is large. We suspect that there are no other guests. Every now and then – sometimes very early in the morning – we hear the distant whine of a vacuum cleaner on another floor. Who are they vacuuming for? They never vacuum for us. We lie on our beds, stifling in the thick air, rubbing at our sticky eyes. The windows do not open. I decide it is sinister that the windows do not open. After the broken key tag situation it is hard for me to trust the hotel staff. Perhaps the room is bugged. They have our passports, after all. Every night I expect to come back to some fresh damage and another bill for repair. A hole punched in the wall, possibly a broken chair. The suffocating heat does not diminish my unease.

Dear Alicia, I write on a postcard to my sister, We are having a wonderful time in Prague and looking after our hotel room very well. The Czech hospitality is marvellous.

I hand it to the receptionist to post. I smile at her. Diky, post, please, I say. You post?, nodding – Stamp? Diky.

Don't shout, hisses Hal from behind me. You'll ruin everything. You post, I say, please, diky, read it, you silly slav cow, diky.

We make a new friend at the Globe. His name is Dick and he's American. A New Yorker, he tells us, but will later under the influence of vodka admit he is from 'Joisey'. Dick and Hal play backgammon while I write letters I will never send, and drink tumblerfuls of red wine, and listen. Dick's just been in Vietnam.

Oh yeah, he says, it was beautiful. Like going back in time, man. This incredible French architecture, women in long silk pants. Unbelievably cheap, you know, everything. He snickers.

And I mean everything.

Hal snickers too. I look at the rain on the Globe's windows and try to imagine Saigon.

We take Dick back to our hotel, where I get changed, and on to the Whale Bar. Vodka, vodka, we cry. Dick pays for everything in American money. In Vietnam, he tells us, he decided to become a dong millionaire. He exchanged however many hundred US dollars into Vietnamese dong, until he had a suitcase filled with great bricks of money. He kept the million dong locked in this suitcase in his hotel room for a week, not touching it. Then he got crazy on Long Island Iced Tea one night after this little Spanish señorita he'd been going with left town. He gambled every last bit of the money away, ha ha ha, playing poker and 21.

I challenge him to a game of 21, feeling lucky because it's my age and besides I'm rather good at it, but Hal cuts in and says I'm not allowed. Dick and Hal both smile at me, like older brothers, like members of the same team. What can I do?

Czech chicks! Czech chicks! Hal is getting desperate. It is difficult for him, travelling with me in tow. He accuses me of sabotaging all his flirtatious encounters. I can't help it. Mostly I try not to, but sometimes when he goes to the bathroom I look at the girl he's been eyeing up and I give her the evils. I'm only protecting him from himself, after all. Things got nasty once, in Warsaw. Hal fell in with a bad crowd, turpentine, death metal, etcetera, and I had to bail him out. This short Polack girl glommed onto us and wouldn't leave our hotel. Crying, carrying on. Baby, she kept saying, baby. Either it was the only English she knew or it was a serious accusation. Some meat-faced guy who said he was her brother turned up on the scene, ranting and raving. Hal didn't like the idea of a big Polish wedding so we shoved some cigarettes at them and split town. I'm not ready to leave Prague yet, so Hal will just have to keep himself in hand. Ha ha ha.

Petrin Hill. What a climb! The heels on my boots stick into the earth and I skid on wet leaves. Hal has to drag me up most of the way while Dick strides on ahead. By the time we're at the top my arms are only just still in their sockets. Something awful happens. Hal doubles over outside the observatory. It could be his back problem. Or it could be liver failure. It makes a good photograph. Aaoow, he says, aaoow. I say cheese while Dick clicks the camera. Tears come out of Hal's eyes. I hold his hands. I feel that I should because some nights he sits on the edge of his bed while I sit on the edge of mine and he holds my hands. (Those are the nights I can't breathe or speak, the nights when the world is spinning way too fast and giving me the shakes. Vodka and cigarettes fail to stop these shakes any more but Hal holding my hands sometimes helps.) It doesn't seem the same rule applies to his back pain. Aaoow, aaoow. Poor baby. I make him lie flat on the damp ground and wipe the sweat off his face. I look around for Dick but he's not there. Help, I shout to the passers-by, *Au secours!* They keep on passing by. Hal pants and whimpers some more. It hurts to watch him. Then Dick reappears with a hip-flask of whisky. Hal drinks some and shuts his eyes and smiles. His whimpering subsides. He gets to his feet and laughs. What a relief! We love Dick! We jump around. We run all over the top of the hill taking photographs of each other. We are a music video.

Franz Kafka was one skinny guy. Kind of good-looking though. Huh, says Hal, you think so?

He thinks I'm shallow. To prove him wrong I buy a copy of *The Trial*. I will read it soon, right after I've finished *Laughable Loves*.

Dick has hours of fun reading the Police Service note on his street map. 'Dear friends,' he shouts to us in a cod Czech accent as we walk up to meet him outside the usual place, 'for the answer to your question, how the crime in Prague differs from the crime in other European cities, it is possible to say: in no way!'

Or, hysterically, in Whale he will tell the barman, 'In the number of committed criminal acts counted for 100,000 inhabitants the Czech Republic is in the order after the Netherlands, Germany, Austria and Switzerland. Therefore Prague is a quiet oasis basically.'

He has memorised it. Hal groans and wrinkles his nose but I could listen to it over and over again.

Dick also likes to remind us that, 'Prague has street prostitutes, too. You can see them in Prelova Street and in a part of Narodni Street. We do not recommend to contact them.'

Hal and Dick have left me alone! Meanies. They've gone 'out on the town' and didn't let me go with them. You better not leave the hotel, they said to me. It's not safe for a young girl alone in the big city.

Life is a cabaret, old chum, they sing as they swing down the stairs of the hotel, leaving me standing forlorn in the doorway, calling out, We do not recommend to contact them. We do NOT recommend it.

I go to Whale, I go to Roxy.

At Roxy I am drinking vodka and not dancing. I am wearing tight Lycra and am highly groomed in order to stand out from the babydoll T-shirts, grubby denim and ornamental hairclips around me. I look fantastique. A boy of I guess about 17 makes eyes at me. I make eyes back. Then I ignore him, kind of cool. He walks past me. He has a nice body. He turns and smiles at me. I smile back. He walks back past me the other way. I laugh into my vodka. He beckons me to come and sit with him and his friends. I saunter over.

Hi, I say.

Hi, they say. One of them lights my cigarette.

Are you having becher? says the one about to go to the bar. They are Czech! This is perfect. It is cultural relations. Foreign affairs. They buy me drinks even though the money I nicked from Hal's secret supply at the hotel would probably pay their rent for a month. They are economics students.

After the revolution, the one who is still making eyes at me explains, we all wanted to be businessmen. Yuppies. They laugh at this, and I laugh too. Now they would all rather be poets. It is more romantic. But they've enrolled in their courses and they must finish them, or their parents would be disappointed. They ask me what I do and I tell them nothing. They are jealous. They are stoned.

This grass, my boyfriend says, is extra strong. Do you know why? It is because of the acid rain that rained down on all the plants after Chernobyl. The acid gets into the dope and makes it extra strong.

I stifle a yawn.

The friends go to dance and leave me alone with my boyfriend. He has a beautiful smile and a slow blink so I kiss him.

That'll show Hick and Dal.

The Hunger Wall. So-called because at the time it was built there was great poverty. Those men who worked on the wall were guaranteed food. Therefore they did not go hungry. Therefore it was a good thing to heave boulders up to the top of Petrin Hill for days on end. Without machinery or anything. Oh! it is too sad. Aaoow. We carve our initials into one of the rocks with my boyfriend's Swiss Army Knife. It is a gesture of solidarity.

Prague 3 contains student accommodation. I know this because I spend a night there, even though I am no student. I stay in the dorm, in an empty room vacated by a friend of my boyfriend's for the night. We stay there together and I wish I could remember more of it but the truth is I don't. I do remember that he says, You are the first older woman I am with (he is 18; I am 21). He also says, I suppose you have read *Unbearable Lightness of Fucking Being*. And, When I have a girlfriend my studies go well and my room is tidier. He spent last summer in New York – actually in Queens, working in a Greek restaurant. It did not improve his English. He says, I know the black slang – fuck you, motherfucker. I laugh. He is nice. He is sweet. He blinks slowly and he waits for a taxicab with me in the morning. You should take the tram, he says, which is a million kroner cheaper than a taxi, but I have never taken a tram in this city before and I am not going to start now. It is enough of a struggle to get back to where the hotel is and find Hal and Dick without this tram business. He kisses me goodbye and I cry in the taxicab because I am lost and he was nice and sweet and I am not sure where I am going to find Dick and Hal and what sort of mood they will be in when finally I do.

Places where Hal and Dick are not. They are not at the hotel. They are not at Globe. They are not at FX. I think I see them on Charles Bridge but it is not them, just two Australians who look worried when I cry. I have to find them. Whale. Globe. FX. I even go to Chapeau Rouge but it's too early and there's nobody there but the bar staff and a girl smoking a pipe. (It is a good look, and one to consider adopting later.) Where could they be? I ring the hotel and when the receptionist hears me talking she hangs up. I am lost in a city where I don't speak the language and I can't find my only two friends in the whole world. This must be the price of casual sex – my 18-year-old, whose name I didn't ever quite hear properly. I need somebody to hold my hands.

In Vietnam, Dick told us, there are beggars who bang their heads on the ground, harder and harder until you pay them to stop.

In Chapeau Rouge again I find them. They have not been back to the hotel. They are still on their bender. Welcome to the lost weekend, they tell me. You naughty, naughty girl, what are you doing out of your room? Dick has two Swedish girls on his arm and Hal is sulking. He is out of Marlboros and is smoking the local brand which he complains is ripping his throat to shreds. Dick has been beating him at backgammon, drinking and girls. I tell them what I've been doing and they berate me for half an hour about the dangers of unknown boys, unknown drugs, unknown addresses and unprotected sex. I didn't mean to tell them about that bit but I'm so happy to have found them I don't care.

Don't care was made to care, Hal tells me.

Yes, says Dick. Don't care was hung.

We have to see Dick to the airport. I don't like city airports, always on the edge of town past flat rust-coloured buildings and low trees. I don't like seeing so much asphalt all in one place. Big airport hotels. Hangars, and shuttle buses. Rental car places. Corrugated iron manufacturers. I know it's not fashionable to think nature is beautiful and that these man-made monstrosities are a waste of space. You're so un-modern, Hal will say. This is the future, this is real. You are such a girl.

We all cry a little, saying goodbye. Well, we make the sounds of crying and that's enough. Dick is going to Kingston, Jamaica. My heart is down, he sings, My head is spinning around.

But that's the leaving Kingston song, I say, not the leaving Prague song.

There is no leaving Prague song, he says, because I am too bowed with grief for music.

Oh, I sigh, and feel a single tear running down my cheek.

Huh, says Hal.

Goodbye, says Dick.

Au revoir! Au revoir!

To comfort ourselves we take a walk by the river. It is grey, and glimmering (it never stops glimmering). We see a man fishing down a grating with a hat out to collect money. There is slightly too much of this sad-eye clown culture in Prague, if you ask me. Paintings on velvet, puppets on string – that sort of thing.

Take my picture, I tell Hal.

I pose next to the fishing clown and look mournful. We have six rolls of black-and-white film. It is *très romantique*. Me on the Charles Bridge, me with the Vltava in the background, me in front of the cathedral. *Très* Juliette Binoche. We don't take photographs of Hal. *Il est trop laide*. We did take some of Dick, Dick and me in pornographic contortions in our hotel room. We can sell them to the taxi drivers if we ever run out of money. This won't happen. Not as long as we stay in Eastern Europe.

What are you feeling, Hal asks me, surprisingly, back at the hotel. What are you feeling? F.e.e.l.i.n.g.

I shrug, giggling.

Search me!

Hal can sniff out an exhibition opening at 20 paces, in any city. They are the same the world over, unlike poetry readings. The tricky part is timing it so's you're not conspicuous out-of-towners, but not getting there so late that all the free drink is gone. We throw back as much as we can, look at the art a bit, and leave. This show involves a lot of perspex and fluorescent light. It's conceptual.

We don't understand the concept. There is a cultural divide.

Hal is losing patience with my spouting of inside knowledge of the Czech people, gleaned from the night I spent with my sex slav. He accuses me of trying to make the best of a botched situation. Yes?, I say, not sure quite what is wrong with that. It comes out that he is still cross with me for doing it, that he thinks I took a stupid risk, that he believes 'it's different for girls,' ie worse, and that as he's responsible for me I should respect his wishes. Then he actually says, 'act your age not your shoe size'. Excuse me? Hello? He can't tell me to grow up. I'm 21. I am grown up! But I do shut up, mainly because I've repeated everything the sex slav and his friends told me and everything I've read in *Laughable Loves* (which after all is fiction, and quite old) and I've run out of inside knowledge about the Czech culture. Damn.

I miss Dick. No amount of cajoling or wheedling would persuade him to delay his ticket. Have I been let down by him? Yes. Has he used me? It's dawning on me that, most probably, he has. It's not that I thought it was love or anything, I just felt like – we had a special bond. The time when we snuck away from Hal and ate sausages in Wenceslas Square, and Dick said that Prague was the most romantic city in the world and I held my breath, then had to let it out after a minute because nothing happened... The times when I'm sure I caught him looking at me in a certain kind of way... The enthusiasm he showed for our dirty photo session...I could have been wrong. I must have been too gullible. I have no instinct about Dick. Perhaps I'll get back to the hotel and find a one-way ticket to Jamaica waiting for me. It's possible, after all; anything is possible!

I can see myself marrying someone like Dick – I can imagine the wedding, the honeymoon, the drink and the infidelities. The reconciliations, the antidepressants, the children and the diets. The trial separations, the therapy. Dick reminds me of Robert Wagner. The glamour.

Huh, says Hal, when I confess my marital fantasy over vodkas at HP (a mistake, both the venue and the confession), You've been

Emily Perkins

reading too many novels. And now I am confused because the old argument used to be that I didn't read enough! Hal is hard to please. I tell him so – it seems to please him.

How long is it since I've seen the sea? I wake up, adrenaline racing through me. Hal, I say, Hal, how far away from the ocean are we? He snores and rolls over. We have a map. I dig it out of the suitcase and spread it over my bed. In the faint light I can make out where we are. Then Hungary, Romania, Black Sea. Austria, Italy, Adriatic Sea. Germany, Netherlands, North Sea. Poland, Baltic Sea – the shortest route. We're surrounded on all sides. The room is extra hot. My hands are prickling. I don't want the river. I don't want some dead old spa town or a lake. I want the ocean, the Pacific Ocean. The new world. This neverending stone oppresses me. The cobbled streets, the ruins, the ancient tombs – it's all so much dust. You can have it. It smells like decay and chalk. Boulders being carried up mountains. Wake up, Hal, wake up.

Hey, says Hal, I know. Let's change all our money and become zloty millionaires. Ha ha ha.

I'd rather be travelling with the fishing clown than be travelling with this. I mean it.

I thought I saw Dick today, in the little cafe, on the steps above the castle. We'd been looking at the tomb of Vladimir the Torturer, or whatever his name is. Again. Crypt after crypt, monument after monument, one fascinating piece of history after another. The guy I thought was Dick was actually the tour guide. You never know.

An old American man who has been hitting on me follows us out of Chapeau Rouge. Gross. He's 40 at least. He totters along the street after us while we giggle, ignoring him. He's muttering something. We stop so we can hear what it is. He catches up with us, looks confused as if he's trying to remember where he knows us from. I lean towards him, into the mutter.

Is Roxy open. Is Roxy open. Is Roxy open.

This is what he has to say.

We walk through Unpronounceable Square for breakfast at

220

Cornucopia.

What do you want to do today? asks Hal.

Go to the beach, I say.

Ha ha ha.

We go shopping. I buy a beret and Hal buys a fridge magnet, though we do not own a fridge. We walk up to the Globe, we read English magazines and play backgammon. We drink coffee and all the time I'm thinking the sea, the sea. The white light of home, the smell of salt and coconut oil, hot rubber and woodsmoke. Summer music from a car stereo. Roller blades and pohutukawa flowers, green hills and the green horizon of the sea.

You are as drunk as a rainbow. That's another thing the sex slav said to me, that I'd forgotten. I'm not quite sure what it means – only, I suppose (an educated guess) that you are very, very drunk.

I am sick in the toilet at Roxy. I splash my face with cold water the way men do and tell myself it's only motion sickness.

'Pickpockets,' Dick was fond of telling me, 'prefer to work in a tight squeeze. It arises especially in department stores.' Then he'd kiss my cheek. Just remember that, honey, he'd say, they like nothing more than a tight squeeze. Ha ha ha. Diky, Dick.

Do you understand, says Hal, holding my hands in the hot hotel room, that we can't go back yet?

My teeth are chattering.

Look at me, he says. Do. You. Understand.

He waits. I nod my head, yes.

OK, he says. OK. Tomorrow we'll take the train to Budapest. Smile!

We go to Budapest. We go.

221

OLD TOAD ON A BIKE
SIMON GANDOLFI

Englishman Simon Gandolfi lives in the Hereford-shire countryside with his wife and two sons. He has fictionalised his travels for some 40 years in a dozen novels published in as many languages. He has turned finally to travel writing in his mid-70s with a planned trilogy covering three motorcycle journeys. Completed in 2008, the first two, on a Honda 125, took him from Veracruz, Mexico, to Tierra del Fuego and back north to New York. For the third he is riding round India, again on a Honda 125, and plans celebrating his 77th birthday basking in the pool at one of the fabulous Taj Mahal spa hotels. You can find Simon online at www .simongandolfi.com.

I AM IN EL BOLSÓN, a small mountain town in Argentine Patagonia. I am 74 years old and overweight. I should be back home in Herefordshire, England, dead-heading roses, concocting an acceptable excuse for not mowing the lawn or collecting a teenage son from the train station. I am riding a small motorbike for the length of the Americas. How small? A Honda 125 – the original pizza-delivery bike. It's the maximum weight my legs would support, and I didn't want a big bike anyway: they erect a wealth barrier and colour people's perception of who you are. I am here for the people: how they live, their beliefs, their thoughts, their hopes of a better future.

'It's something you need to do,' my wife said. 'It's what you've always wanted to do. Go and get young again and write me a good book.'

I bought the bike new in Veracruz, Mexico: my starting point is the first house Cortez built and from which he set out to conquer Mexico. My goal is grander. I have been riding south for the past six months. Central America was easy. Distances were manageable; so was the climate. In the south you freeze on the Altiplano and ride 150 kilometres for a cup of coffee. For altitude, 4700 metres is my record – that was in Bolivia – and I've put 22,000 kilometres on the clock.

Pine forest and snowcapped mountains surround El Bolsón. It is a tourist town. Restaurants, hotels and hostels abound. The buildings are mostly wood – or pretending to be wood. Switzerland and Austria do it better. I have stayed two nights gathering strength for the ride south through Patagonia to Ushuaia in Tierra del Fuego. Distances are vast, so I leave at first light. I am dressed in two pairs of long johns, two pairs of pyjama trousers, cargo pants, three undervests, two long-sleeved shirts, three jerseys, a leather bomber jacket, three pairs of socks and brown leather Church's shoes. I have stuffed two newspapers down my front, wrapped a scarf round my face and wear two pairs of gloves and a blue rain-suit. Imagine a large blue balloon.

The road from El Bolsón climbs out of a wooded valley to open moors, where a few sheep cringe among sparse tufts of coarse grass. The clouds are black and I ride through thin flurries of snow. Two cops wrapped in frost-retardant suits and balaclavas shelter beside a pick-up. I ask what happened to the central heating. One cop says, 'The Government forgot to pay the gas bill.'

Esquel was a hippie haven in the '70s. Now it is a fashionable resort – intelligent hippies tracked the change, became entrepreneurs and now shop with platinum-grade credit cards. The less intelligent continue to roll herbal cigarettes, throw the I Ching or ponder tarot cards. I top up with petrol and head for Tecka.

The road follows a wide, flat river valley of huge sheep paddocks. Skinny trees grow along the river. I startle a flight of green parrots. What are parrots doing up here on the Altiplano? And why haven't the farmers planted shelter strips? Shelter would improve the pasture.

Tecka doesn't look much on the Auto Club map. So much for maps: Tecka holds a treasure. I turn off the highway onto a dirt street. Tin-roofed bungalows are sealed tight against wind and swirling dust. Half a dozen pick-ups are parked outside a petrol station. The petrol station has been out of use for years: the drivers are here for Sunday lunch at the petrol station cafe.

A true restaurateur is a miracle you happen upon in the strangest places. Evidence starts with the greeting. Tecka, the owner has been waiting all his life for my arrival. Will the *plat du jour* suffice? A simple gnocchi?

Simple? The gnocchi are al dente. The sauce is a combination of tomato, spring onion, garlic, herbs, country ham and Italian sausage. The quantity is as vast as Argentina. It is served in a dish cradled in a basket. It is divine. So are the fresh-baked bread rolls. The sugar on a *crème catalane* is caramelised to perfection. The owner is the chef. A fringe of grey hair surrounds his bald pate. He wears a striped apron and beams as he insists I drink a small grappa for the road. Bikers, forget your schedules. Stop here and eat.

I ride out of Tecka into a full gale. A moment's inattention and I would be slammed off the road. I consider turning back. It was a great restaurant – maybe there is a great bed. However Patagonia is famous for its winds. What I consider a gale is probably the standard Patagonian breeze. Hills on the eastern horizon glow topaz blue. Fifteen guanacos stand on a ridge. I passed a stunted tree 10 kilometres back.

Gobernador Costa is a further 60 kilometres southeast on Route 40. The streets are empty. Those out for a Sunday stroll have been blown away. I stop for petrol and a coffee. A pretty young woman operates both the petrol pump and the espresso machine. She asks where I am going.

'Sarmiento,' I say.

'That's 260 kilometres,' she says.

I agree.

'There's a gale blowing,' she says.

I've noticed.

'You should stay the night here,' she says.

'Patagonia is famous for wind', I say. 'Will there be less wind tomorrow?'

'Of course there will be less,' she says. 'This is a storm. We don't always have storms.'

She fails to convince me. There could be a storm tomorrow. It could bring a more intense wind. If I weaken, I could be stuck here for weeks. I don't have weeks. I want to be home for my eldest son's birthday.

I wrap the scarf round my face, and pull on my two pairs of gloves. The road runs straight as a ruler over undulating moorland. A black dot in the distance becomes a truck. I crouch low over the petrol tank. Wind buffets as we pass. I recognise a face watching me over a fence. He is a young chap, not fully grown, not too shy. I park and dismount – no easy manoeuvre for an overweight balloon.

'Where are you from?' he asks.

'Colwall,' I reply.

'In Herefordshire? That's close to Ledbury.'

'Ten kilometres,' I say.

'I believe that's where my great-great-grandfather came from,' he tells me.

'Very probably,' I say and take his photograph.

He is embarrassed at having spent so much time with an old fogey. Off he trots to join his friends.

I hunt through layers of clothes and manage a piss downwind. I tell myself that fatigue is merely a state of mind. I have no grounds for complaint. By profession I am a novelist. For years I have lived in other people's heads. I longed to live my own life for a while, live my own adventure. I swing my leg over the saddle at the third attempt. The motor starts first kick. It's 150 kilometres to Sarmiento. Brmmm-brmmm…

The road dips through hills reminiscent of the Scottish borders. Wind and weather have rounded every crest. The lee side of a hill has collapsed. A curved pink cliff rises above the fallen waves of grassed earth. Wild geese face west into the wind. The nearest pollution must be hundreds of kilometres to the north. I am struck by the clarity of light and the extraordinary depth of blue in the sky. The blue is reflected in the lake on the approach to Sarmiento. The lake at Villa del Chocon was the same amazing blue. So was Lake Titicaca. I have seen parrots today. I have seen flamingos graze in ponds alongside sheep and Hereford cattle. My awareness that flamingos breed in the Andes fails to make their presence any less surprising. Those long thin legs should freeze and snap.

Now, in the evening, I pass cars parked by a bridge on the outskirts of Sarmiento. Sunday fisherman stroll with fly rods along a sheltered riverbank. I turn off the road at a sign offering bed and breakfast. Dogs greet me kindly. A woman shows me a bunkroom with six beds and use of a kitchen that she rents out for $20. I don't have use for six bunks; nor can I use the kitchen. My logic confronts her prices. My logic fails. I take a room in town at the Hotel Ismir for $15. The room is miserable, so am I. I have ridden 600 kilometres. I am exhausted and have hay fever or a streaming head cold.

I shower and walk a couple of blocks in search of a restaurant. Joy deserts Sarmiento in a gale. Bungalows shrink within themselves. People huddle and watch TV. The Hotel Colon is a rarity. I spy six men at the bar. I guess that they missed out on Sunday church service and have been at the bar much of the day. How will they view an intruder, a Brit? I pass half a dozen times before gaining courage to enter. A set of aluminium doors leads into a porch, from where more doors open to the bar. The doors grate and squeak and clatter. An army tank would make less noise. Conversation ends. The six men at the bar turn on their stools and inspect me. So does the owner. So does his wife. I hold my hands above my head in surrender.

'I am a Brit,' I say. 'Am I allowed?'

'They allow horses,' says a man in a flat leather gaucho hat.

The Hotel Colon in Sarmiento is the type of dump any respectable biker hankers after. The bar is the right length: six people and it doesn't feel empty; 12 and it doesn't feel overcrowded. Sarmiento is a small town. I doubt there are more than 12 serious bar-stool occupiers. The six in possession have been on the same conversation for a while. Maybe it began yesterday, or last week or last year. It is one of those conversations that expand over time and develop threads that go nowhere and are put to death. Mostly what is said now alludes to what has been said earlier; you would need to have been in on the conversation from the beginning to understand its direction – if it has a direction.

I sit at the far end of the bar, order a small beer and watch the last few minutes of a football match on TV. The conversationalists seem content with my presence. The pool table to the left of the bar hasn't been used in months. It is there because this type of bar requires a pool table. The girlie beer advertisements exist for the same reason. They are expected, as are the three tables, each with four folding chairs, arranged along the wall. The bar-stool residents would be uncomfortable were they absent.

A young couple occupies the table closest to the door. I guess that they are students. She wears spectacles and is perhaps the more confident – or the more pressing – one in their relationship. The obligatory guitar case protrudes from among the bags and backpacks heaped on the floor. I wonder if they are waiting for a bus – or for a parent. I imagine my teenage sons calling home. 'Dad, can you pick us up?' I wonder if my sons are aware of the happiness it gives me to be asked. To be of use is a joy, no matter the time of day or night. I will bitch, of course. Bitching is expected. I don't ask how many 'us' is. I don't ask if the girl is a friend or a girlfriend. Asking would be an infringement. Of course I want to know – not to judge, but because this is part of who they are. However, I do wish that they would sit a while in the kitchen once we get home, let me cook them something, talk to me, let me share a little of their lives. They tend to hurry straight upstairs to their room. I guess it's my age. I'm sort of odd, an embarrassment. You know? Teenagers with a dad in his seventies. And, yes, I am odd. Riding a pizza-delivery bike through the length of the Americas is odd. And I've dragged them off to live in strange places: they attended state primary school in Cuba for a few years. Nor is writing novels a proper job.

I ask Mrs Hotel Colon if there is a restaurant open nearby. She asks whether a steak and fries would satisfy. A steak and fries would be just dandy. I drink a second beer and nod intelligently to asides from my bar-stool neighbours. The asides refer to the general conversation. A mystic would find them obtuse. Mrs Hotel Colon summons me to a small dining room. She says, 'I put a couple of eggs on your steak.' I thank her and ask for a third beer. I take my place back at the bar. One of the stools nods to the owner. The owner places a small glass of clear liquid fire in front of me. I raise my glass in gratitude. The conversation continues. I am blissfully content.

Three beers and dinner cost $7. The room rate for a single with bath is $15. Should you ever pass through Sarmiento, you know where to stay. Take a right at the park, ride three blocks and turn left. The Colon is on your right. Don't bother with the conversation. It won't be comprehensible. You are a year or two late…

ON THE TRAIL OF THE CASPIAN TIGER

TIM CAHILL

Tim Cahill is the author of innumerable magazine articles and nine books, the most recent of which is *Hold the Enlightenment: More Travel, Less Bliss.* He is the co-author of the IMAX film *Everest* and two other Academy Award–nominated motion pictures. He lives in Montana.

SAIM GÜCLÜ WAS TO BE our minder. We imagined that he'd report back to the government of Turkey about our movements and our motives. We'd contracted for our own driver, but the various government agencies had become intransigent: Saim would be our man, we'd travel with him, in his car, with a driver supplied by him, and the privilege would cost us petrol plus US$300 a day if we took pictures in any national park. People were shooting one another in the national parks we needed to visit and the roads to them were lined with military checkpoints. We weren't going to get through any of them without our official minder.

So we waited for Saim at a hotel on Lake Van, in southeastern Turkey. And while we waited, I reviewed my notes, concentrating on the comments of a number of foreign correspondents for major news organisations.

'Ha ha ha,' is what they had said to us in Istanbul, or words to that effect.

'You will,' they had assured us, 'never get to the southeast area of the country.' This was in early December of 2000, and there were the remnants of a revolution going on there at the time: the Marxist PKK (Kurdish Workers Party) was engaged in intermittent skirmishes with the Turkish military. As a result, Turkish officials were not allowing journalists into the area. A BBC crew had been expelled only a week ago, as had an American journalist who'd ventured a bridge too far.

In the following days, as we sat in offices in Istanbul and Ankara seeking travel permits from numerous agencies, I got the impression that while Turkish officials expressed deep concern for our safety in the area, this was not a paramount issue. I believed that these fine administrators did not want to read another journalistic effort which made the Kurds out to be a swell ethnic minority oppressed by the evil Turks. This article had been written so many times that it even had a name: the Cuddly Kurd Terrible Turk story.

But we – myself, writer Thomas Goltz and photographer Rob Howard – were not going into this sensitive area to write about the ongoing insurrection. Oh no. We were going in under what many of our colleagues thought was the most laughable cover story ever devised. 'You think anyone will seriously believe that you are looking for a tiger?' they asked us.

'They will believe us,' I said, 'because we are pure of heart.'

'Then you buy the next round and we'll tell you why it's not going to happen.'

The borders with Iran and Iraq, in the mountainous southeastern part of the country where we wanted to go, were particularly hot at this time. There had, for instance, just been a shoot-out in the town of Semdinli. Unfortunately, our research suggested that this was the area where we were most likely to find traces of the Caspian tiger, a huge beast, almost three metres from nose to tail, and the second biggest tiger on earth, after the Siberian species. The Caspian tiger wasn't just elusive; it was considered to be extinct. The last one had supposedly been shot in the southern Turkish town of Uludere in 1970. Now Turkish conservation groups were hearing scattered reports of tiger sightings on the border of Iraq, where Turks and revolutionary Kurds had been shooting at one another for 16 years. We thought we'd go take a look. What could possibly go wrong?

Saim Güclü, as it turned out. Our instructions, from the offices of the military and the media, said that Saim would meet us in the town of Van, at the finest of the local hotels, on the shores of the lake that some people say was the original Garden of Eden. The lobby was deserted, but Saim arrived right on time, just about noon. He was a big, well-fed man in his early sixties, dressed for a tiger hunt in a sports jacket and jumper, and he walked with that delicate grace often seen in full-bellied men. He smiled incessantly, in a way that was so sincerely merry I felt subtly menaced. The smile lived under a full and extravagant white moustache.

Saim said that he was the Chief Engineer of the National Forest in this area of eastern Anatolia. He did not fit my image of a ranger. This was definitely not a guy who could keep up with the rest of us on foot. I wondered if we could ditch him, or if that would lead to our arrest and expulsion.

It was too late to start for tiger country: the sun would set by four on this December day. We were in the lower latitudes, yes, but Turkey doesn't divide itself into time zones, reasoning, I think, that such separations might give citizens secessionist ideas. Consequently, if we left immediately, we would be passing through military checkpoints in the dark – which is sometimes a fatal notion and certainly not a good idea under any circumstance.

We decided to spend the afternoon visiting an island in Lake Van where there were the remains of a 4th-century Armenian church. The lake was blue under a crisp sky and snow glittered on the mountains above. If Adam and Eve had spent the entire year here naked, they were a couple of tough monkeys. The temperature hovered right around freezing.

The church was adorned with various friezes: Saint George and the dragon, Cain and Abel, and Moses, among others. At the base of the Byzantine dome, there were depictions of animals. The tiger was the most prominent of these creatures. Rob shot some photos.

'Ha,' Saim said, in his merry way, 'now you pay three hundred dollars.' Was he serious?

'Yeah, ha ha,' I said.

Somehow the idea of the tiger was receding rapidly in my mental rear-view mirror. Perhaps I could salvage something of the story by doing a quick piece about the Van cat. This is a creature that looks like an ordinary fuzzy white Persian cat except that one eye is blue and the other is green. There was a hideous poured concrete sculpture of just such a cat with her kitten on the highway entering Van. The coloured eyes glittered oddly out of the grey concrete. Rob shot a few pictures and Saim said, 'Three hundred dollars.'

'Right.' But now the sun was going down and we needed to get across town quick, to the university, where there was a Van

cat genetic conservation program going on in a building called
the Kedi Evi, literally the 'Cat House'. It was Ramadan and pious
Muslims had been fasting and refraining from drinking water all
day. When the sun set, the feast was on. We bashed through traffic in Saim's forestry truck, racing Ramadan to the Cat House.

It was a two-storey building on the shores of Lake Van, all
done up rather elegantly in polished hardwoods. A young man
named Mehmet Atarbayir met us at the door, which was festooned with signs reading: 'We are animals. We are an essential
part of nature, please don't kill us. In other countries, our relatives
are happy but in the heaven that is Turkey it is wrong to make us
animals live in hell.'

Mehmet Atarbayir was in a kind of hell at that moment. It
was his job to show us about and his dinner was only 10 minutes away. He escorted us into the central courtyard, which was
fenced. There were a few kittens playing among the wild flowers in the grass growing under a giant skylight. Down the long
hallway there was a series of doors with large windows in them.
Behind the windows there were furnished rooms – radiators and
old couches and bookshelves and dressers. Stretched out and loll-
ing about on all this furniture were any number of odd-eyed Van
cats. They looked like feline versions of Salvador Dali's melted
clocks.

I interviewed Mehmet, who was so hungry his brain couldn't
get out of low gear. Were the cats intelligent? Yes. How did he
know? He just did. What did they do? Couldn't I see what they
did? What happened when Mehmet went into the rooms? The
cats sat on his lap and purred.

Mehmet, probably contemplating dinner, was hustling us out
the front door just as the sun set and I was reduced to asking the
most moronic of journalistic questions. 'What,' I said, 'is the fun-
niest thing that ever happens in the Van Cat House?'

The young man drew himself up to his full height and said,
'I would never say anything to demean my charges, the cats.' He
said this with such obvious sincerity and respect that I squelched

a huge burst of laughter bubbling up in my chest. I glanced at Saim. He had turned his back and was faking a series of coughs. Mehmet felt the necessity to restate his answer: 'Nothing funny ever happens in the Van Cat House,' he said angrily.

And we all burst into laughter. Saim fell into my arms and we hooted helplessly for some time, two hefty guys holding one another and shaking. From a distance, we might have looked like men mourning a fallen comrade.

The cats in the Cat House broke our mutual distrust. Over the next few weeks we became colleagues, then friends. Saim was, in fact, a ranger, but the wildlife section of the forestry department had only been established in 1994. The Kurdish insurrection had started eight years before. No one from forestry had been in the southeast area to inventory animals. 'This is exciting for me,' Saim said. 'But I am ashamed to say that this is work we should have done years ago.'

Saim was able to talk us through several of the checkpoints that had stymied our journalistic colleagues. We were deeper into Turkey than any foreigners had been in some time. In between searches at the checkpoints, Saim and I talked tigers.

We were meeting men in towns like Semdinli who swore they'd seen tracks. Saim had them describe these tracks and draw them in a notebook. There were lynx and a kind of Anatolian panther in the mountains and Saim didn't want to make any mistakes. It was a sad irony that the animals – the tigers and goats and bears – were coming back in the areas where the fighting was the most fierce, where the trails were mined and it was risking your life to be seen in the forest with a rifle. No one had hunted the area in 16 years. And now the animals were coming back. Even, it appeared, the tiger.

In Semdinli, a Turkish Army colonel listened to Saim and apologised that we couldn't walk the forest, searching for scat. However, he did allow us to go on a military manoeuvre which involved armoured personnel carriers and several dozen armed Kurdish village guards, allied with the Turks. In the towns along the border with Iraq, we met with folks who knew the mountains. There was some controversy, but enough people had had encounters with something very like a tiger that I was becoming convinced it still existed. Saim thought so, too. 'I'm about 50 per cent certain they are still up there in the mountains,' he said.

In Uludere, where the last known Caspian tiger had been shot, the subgovernor, whom Saim later called a 'son of a goat', threatened to confiscate our film. It was best to simply flee. Saim herded us into the forestry truck and we went speeding off down the highway, past a small picturesque village of houses built from river rock. The town was deserted and only parts of the stone walls still stood. The whole place had been demolished by field artillery. Saim stared at the devastation, in a place where Turkey could have been heaven. His face coloured and a vein stood out on his forehead. He said, 'Whoever did this to these people – the military or the revolutionaries – may Allah strike them blind.' Which was my feeling on the matter as well.

We fled south and west, along the border with Iraq, and parted in the city of Sirnac, which was protected by a checkpoint manned by obstinate soldiers who decided the Americans should be imprisoned until officers had a chance to interrogate us. This did not sound like any fun at all and Saim worked his magic, talking to more and more senior officers until he found one who was intrigued by the idea that an extinct tiger still existed in the mountains surrounding us. 'Go,' the officer said. 'Don't let anyone see you in Sirnac. I do this for the tiger.'

We parted in that city, Saim and I. The forestry truck was parked in front of a sweet shop where Thomas, Rob and I found a driver willing to take us to the Iraq border. We transferred our gear, then I hugged Saim and he kissed my cheeks, thrice, in the Turkish manner. He would not take the money that we owed him.

'The tiger,' he said, 'does not belong to Turkey or America or Iraq. We do this for the world.'

'Yeah, but Saim,' I said, 'we owe you a couple of thousand dollars.'

He shook his head and smiled his merry smile. 'The tiger,' he said, 'is without price.'

A crowd was beginning to gather about us as we argued. Bad news. On this trip, in this area of Turkey, every time we had attracted a crowd – in Uludere, in Semdinli – the police had come quickly. Within minutes. And we definitely weren't supposed to be in Sirnac. We had maybe two minutes until the cops came and put us in a cell to await interrogation.

Saim used our trepidation. 'Go,' he said, in his kind way. And that is what we did, feeling that we owed more than money to the Turkish ranger.

SECRETS OF THE MAYA
LAURA RESAU

Laura Resau's novels *What the Moon Saw, Red Glass,* and *The Indigo Notebook* are set in Latin America, where she has worked and travelled extensively. She now lives in Colorado with her family, and spends most days in a little silver trailer in her driveway, writing and dreaming up excuses for another trip. Please visit her on the web at www.LauraResau.com.

THROUGH MOONLIT FOG, I walked from the bus station towards the colonial *centro* of San Cristóbal, Chiapas. I glimpsed rooms glowing yellow behind thin curtains, shops laced with tiny white lights, restaurants strung with red lanterns. My dog-eared *Maya Cosmos* book, nestled in my backpack, portrayed this southern Mexican state as a land drenched in ancient symbols, only a veil of colonialism cloaking age-old rituals. Fluent in Spanish and armed with a degree in anthropology, I was on a break from the university where I taught in the neighbouring state of Oaxaca. For months I'd been devouring books on Maya spirituality in anticipation of this trip. As a little girl, I'd dreamt of entering magical realms, and now, as a 24-year-old, I longed to discover one of the 'portals' that opened to the Otherworld – what my book called the 'Maya road to reality'.

On the first two days of my long weekend, I stuck to the tourist track; this offered interesting sights, but no doorways to the Otherworld. On Sunday, my final day in Chiapas, I decided to head to Tenejapa, a relatively remote Tzeltal Maya village. As my taxi wound up mountain roads, the thick fog turned into a cold drizzle. We passed a hillside lined with towering crosses painted blue and dressed in pine branches, standing as tall as the neighbouring pine trees. Wooden planks were scattered below among smaller crosses, like unhinged, abandoned doors. Despite the gloomy weather, I felt a thrill. I'd read about this place, a Maya graveyard: the planks were portals to the ancestors' dwelling place, where shamans regularly venture.

The taxi dropped me off at the main square in a lush, green valley. On one side was a church, and on the other, a modest, one-storey building that I guessed was the town hall. Verdant hills of corn and coffee rose up behind it. Beyond the square were a few blocks of low, tile-roofed houses. No market stalls or heaps of fruits or vegetables could be seen, only some clusters of men in ponchos fringed with pink pompoms and women in red-and-black shawls. There was a hopeful pocket of activity in front of the town hall, where about 30 people sat on wooden benches facing each other, women on one end, men on the other.

The men wore hats resembling festive lampshades, dozens of colourful ribbons cascading over the rims. Their outfits were elaborate: red embroidered shorts peeked out beneath the hems of black wool tunics; leather straps were slung over their chests, equipped with knives and canteens made of horn; necklaces of silver medallions hung down past their waists. The older men held staffs that gave them an air of royalty. As I walked towards them, ducking my head in the rain, I noticed their faces were serious, rather closed and unreadable.

The women, at the other end of the benches, seemed more lighthearted. Varying degrees of smile wrinkles fanned out from their eyes. They wore two long braids, dark skirts and white blouses embroidered with tiny red stitches. As they whispered among themselves in Tzeltal, their hands flew over their mouths to suppress their giggles.

'*Buenos dias,*' I said, rubbing my hands together. It was cold enough to see my breath. 'Could you tell me where the tourist office is?'

Two men who appeared to understand Spanish grinned, revealing teeth painted gold and silver. There was a flurry of excitement as they translated for the others.

'No. No tourist office here,' the younger man said.

'What about the market?' I tried.

'What market?'

'Today's market day, right?'

'There is no market here.' They laughed with a metallic flash of teeth.

'Oh,' I felt annoyed at the tour guide who had recommended this place. I was sure he'd said Sunday was market day. 'Thanks anyway.' I turned away awkwardly, aware that the men seemed to be laughing at me, not with me. Well, I thought, I could wander around the town and chat with the women and children; they seemed less intimidating than the horde of ribbon-bedecked men wielding staffs and carrying knives.

The rest of the town was nearly deserted, just a few people on the streets, an occasional dog or burro passing by. I tried, unsuccessfully, to strike up a conversation with three women who smiled apologetically and responded in Tzeltal. This trip was rapidly turning into a failure. With my anthropological detective work thwarted, I was, unfortunately, reduced to a typical obnoxious tourist. Against my better judgment I whipped out my camera.

As I took a few shots of the mountains and the church, I noticed a strange structure – two tree trunks with a beam nailed across. With a wave of excitement, I wondered if this was a variation of the Maya World Tree, the source of all life, the pillar supporting the cosmos.

It occurred to me to ask the ribbon-bedecked men about the tree-cross, but truth be told, they scared me. From a distance I observed them, admiring their zany hats and wishing I could snap their picture. My guide yesterday had warned that many Mayas don't like having their picture taken, since a photo makes them vulnerable to witchcraft. But I had only two more photos left on my roll, so didn't it make sense for me to use them before I left? Chilled to the bone and determined to get something out of this trip, I shrugged off my better instincts and devised a plan: I'd pretend to take a shot of the town hall but secretly zoom in on the lampshade headdresses. I casually wandered closer, feigning interest in far-off mountains, and then nonchalantly raised the camera to my eye. In one furtive gesture, I swung the viewfinder from the peaks over to the town hall and zoomed in. There were the men, in clear focus, looking sternly at me beneath the ribbons, wagging their fingers and shaking their heads.

Caught! I felt a deep blush.

What now? I could run to the road, hope a taxi would pass by soon, go back to San Cristóbal, and pretend this never happened. But I wouldn't be able to live with the shame. I took a long breath and headed towards the group. They stared, their faces grave. I stopped in front of them, aware of all eyes on me.

'*Buenos días,*' I said, feeling my cheeks flush again.

'*Buenos días, señorita,*' they replied.

I launched into a long-winded apology about how deeply sorry I was, how terrible I felt, how really, I didn't usually act like this… 'Please forgive me,' I concluded and held my breath. Would they whip out their knives and pry the film from my camera?

The two men translated for the others, discussed my transgression in low voices, and then burst into laughter. Golden teeth glinted and silver coins jingled. An older man raised his staff. '*Mira, señorita,* you may take pictures of the buildings or mountains, but not of us.'

'Thank you very, very much.' I backed up, half-bowing, embarrassed but relieved. Their laughter followed me as I walked across the wet plaza towards the road. This time they seemed a little gentler, as though they were chuckling at a cute, but pathetic, little kid. When I'd nearly reached the road, my eyes rested on the odd tree-cross structure, and I realised I wasn't ready to give up. I'd already humiliated myself beyond repair. It couldn't get any worse. And after all, this could be my last chance to learn the secrets of Maya reality.

The group watched me walk towards them, their eyebrows raised, amused. 'Uh, *con permiso,*' I said apologetically. 'One more thing. That cross by the church? The one with two tree trunks? What does it symbolise?'

They squinted at the church. They murmured to each other in Tzeltal. They conferred with the women. Were they debating whether to divulge some secret? Was the cross what I suspected – a sacred vestige of the ancient Maya, a portal to the Otherworld?

Finally they announced, 'We don't know what you're talking about.'

I pointed to the cross. 'There,' I insisted. 'See?'

'That thing? That's not a cross. That's what we tie banners to during fiestas.'

'So – there's no deeper meaning?'

They shook their heads. 'No, *señorita.*'

'Oh,' I looked at the rows of faces, ranging from apologetic to entertained. 'Well,' I paused. 'OK then.'

As I turned to go, feeling dejected, a young man said, 'Wait. What's your name, *señorita*?'

'Laura,' I said with a flash of hope. 'And yours?'

'Antonio.'

The other man who spoke Spanish well, Alonso, explained that they were the village authorities and the women were their wives. 'You speak *castellano* very well. Better than us!' Alonso laughed. He offered me a seat on the bench, on the men's side, and we chatted about my hometown of Baltimore, what the weather was like there, what crops we grew, what animals we raised – the usual small talk. Several men began playing beautiful, handmade instruments, variations of mandolins and harps. The melodies were meandering and mysterious, far from the salsa and cumbia tunes I was used to hearing. The group of men and women grew more animated by the minute, darting from Spanish to Tzeltal and back again, voices escalating into waves of laughter.

At some point I became aware of a moustached man standing near me with a shot glass and a bottle of clear liquid. He filled the glass, handed it to a seated man, waited for him to gulp it, and repeated the process with the man beside me. I noticed some of the others, especially the women, glancing at the moustached man and at me, and back at the moustached man. The women looked eager, their eyes full of mischief and hands over their mouths, tittering. Now the moustached man stood in front of me, extending the shot glass freshly filled to the brim.

'What is this?' I asked nervously.

'*Posh*.' He grinned.

'What's *posh*?' I thought of the ubiquitous warning to foreigners: don't drink anything that's not boiled or from a sealed bottle.

'We make it from sugar cane.'

I sniffed it. 'I don't usually drink hard liquor.'

'You must drink it,' Alonso told me with a stern smile.

I hesitated.

'You must drink,' the others echoed, their eyes lit up.

I stared at the shot glass in my lap. It looked unusually big.

Deepening his voice, Antonio said, 'You know what happens to people who don't drink *posh* here?'

'What?'

'We throw them in jail.' This sparked a wave of laughter. 'Yes! We are the village authorities. We say you must drink the *posh*.'

I drank the *posh*. It burned and tingled in my chest, and within minutes, my head was floating. I smiled at everyone, giddy.

Then I caught sight of the moustached man again. He was making another round, this time with a pack of Alitas cigarettes. He walked from person to person, handing each a cigarette. I'd never seen indigenous women smoking before, yet here were 15 of them, taking long drags with gusto. I was not a smoker, but I assumed it was either smoke or go to jail. Trying not to cough, I tentatively took a few puffs.

I bit my lip when the moustached man appeared once again. This time he handed us each a thick glass bottle of Coke, the kind that's been refilled countless times, chipped and scratched and stained. The man opened each Coke ceremoniously. I sipped my Coke politely, grateful for something familiar. Then I noticed the others drinking quickly, filling the air with a cacophony of burping.

The previous day, I'd observed ritual burping inside the church of San Juan Chamula. The church's interior was dark and cavernous, lit by hundreds of tiny candle flames with pine needles scattered over worn floorboards, creating a shadowy forest. Copal incense smoke filled the air; statues of saints lined the walls, adorned with mirrors and flowers; clusters of Maya men and women in traditional dress knelt on the floor, performing spiritual cleansing ceremonies. In one corner, a healer moved a chicken over candle flames, ran it over a sick girl's body to absorb 'evil air', and then snapped the animal's neck. Next she handed the girl a bottle of Pepsi. As she gulped it down and burped, my tour guide murmured, 'She is eliminating the last of the evil air.'

I sipped my Coke with the others, but felt too self-conscious to emit more than a few soft burps. Were we burping out evil air? Was this an elaborate purification ritual? Or were we just, well, drinking and having fun? And I was having fun, warmed by the *posh* and camaraderie, thoroughly relaxed and sinking into the moment. I didn't worry about deeper meaning; it was enough to keep up with the conversation that bounced from coffee consumption to the Zapatista uprising to teenage marriage to Tzeltal verb conjugations to corn cultivation. An unexpected slice of Maya reality.

The moustached man came by again. Now he was passing around a gourd about the size of a fist. Each person poured out a small pile of dried green herb onto their palms, licked it, and passed the gourd on.

'What's that?' I asked Alonso.

'An herb,' he said breezily.

'What's it for?'

He conferred with the others, and a few moments later, came up with, 'It makes you happy.'

Hmmm. I poured some onto my palm and licked. The smell was unfamiliar, definitely not marijuana or any other herb I'd encountered. It tasted like dried grass, and I couldn't distinguish its effects from the alcohol and nicotine and caffeine already coursing through my veins.

After the mysterious herb, the moustached man still wasn't done. Now he circulated with a huge bottle of Superior beer and a single, yellow-flowered glass, the kind I might find in my grandmother's kitchen. He stood like a waiter as each person chugged a beer, and then he moved on to the next. I was never much of a beer-chugger. I took a succession of quick sips, which made the women crack jokes in Tzeltal while the men urged me to drink faster. *'Rápido! Rápido!'*

I finished the beer, laughing along with the others, feeling a proud part of this Maya version of a frat party. I smiled warmly at everyone, the drunken kind of smile that gushed, *Aw, I love you guys!* 'This is a nice fiesta,' I said to Antonio. 'Really communal.'

Antonio grew serious. 'This is not a fiesta. This is a ceremony. This is special, what we're doing now.' He didn't elaborate on its significance, and this time I didn't ask questions, felt no need to analyse it. I just nodded and burped.

When the moustached man came around with more *posh*, I reluctantly declined. I had to get back to San Cristóbal since my bus would depart that evening.

'Stay!' Antonio cried. 'Later there will be a meal and dancing. Spend the night in our home.' The women realised I was leaving and raised their voices in protest. 'Stay!' they repeated in accented Spanish. I shook hands with every single person, saying goodbye in my newly learned Tzeltal. Finally, with a dazed grin, I strolled across the plaza to a taxi that was magically waiting for me.

I never found out what vestiges of ancient Maya rituals, if any, were hidden behind the veil of beer burps and happy herb on my Sunday afternoon in Tenejapa. And in the end, that was fine with me. I had found my own Maya road to reality.

FINDING SHELTER
NICHOLAS CRANE

Nicholas Crane is the author of *Clear Waters Rising, Two Degrees West, Great British Journeys* and *Mercator: The Man Who Mapped the Planet* – the bestselling biography of the world's greatest mapmaker. In recent years, he has presented several TV series for the BBC: *Coast, Map Man, Great British Journeys* and *Nicholas Crane's Britannia*.

THIS STORY – THIS TRUE STORY – concerns reciprocal kindnesses in a country which has come to symbolise humanity's trials. The events took place 20 years ago in the Hindu Kush mountains of Afghanistan, and were recorded in 12 notebooks whose pages were filled by torch light each evening. It's a story which begins and ends in a stone shelter…

We had been in the shelter for half an hour or so when Qudous raised himself into the wind, his shoulders hunched against the cold. As he walked away, his footsteps left a broken line in the snow. He must have realised that we were watching his receding outline because he turned after a few minutes and waved.

The five of us crouched on our haunches, backs to the wall. The shelter was barely waist high. It was set in the centre of a valley, and it caught the force of the wind which gusted down from the pass we had crossed that afternoon. We were tired, hungry, cold and anxious. With scraps of kindling, the two horsemen lit a fire.

Six weeks earlier, we had tramped up this same valley, fit and expectant. The sun had been intense and the grass as soft as velvet. In a mujahedin tent hidden behind the crags above the shelter we now inhabited, we had dozed through the afternoon heat on blankets laid beside an American ground-to-air missile. It was the last summer of the Soviet occupation of Afghanistan and the Cold War was stuttering to a close. For 10 years the Western press had reported on the ragtag bands of horsemen who had held at bay one of the world's two superpowers. Now that superpower was withdrawing from its ill-advised Afghan adventure. In London, the newspapers had been full of conflicting 'pull-out stories': 'Soviet soldiers begin to leave Afghanistan' crowed the front page of the *Daily Telegraph*; 'A dignified retreat' announced the *Independent*; 'Russians set for a scorched earth escape' warned the *Sunday Times* correspondent from Kandahar.

It didn't take a geopolitical genius to grasp that the Soviet departure would not herald the end of Afghanistan's woes. The invaders were leaving a communist regime besieged by several fractious, heavily armed warlords, and they were leaving a homeless population of around eight million. Since 1985, the British private voluntary organisation Afghanaid had been sending small humanitarian teams across the border to Afghanistan with food, medicine and other essential supplies. Through an odd series of circumstances I had become one half of a two-man team charged with evaluating the need for emergency aid among the scattered refugees of the Hindu Kush. Specifically, we were to travel to the Panjshir Valley to monitor the efficacy of the previous year's aid distribution, and to undertake a war-damage survey which would help decision-makers in New York and London to allocate funds for reconstruction.

The job description suited me well: they needed a geographer who could ride a horse and climb mountains. My companion, Julian, was an old Afghan hand, the veteran of several aid trips and the survivor of a close encounter with Soviet gunships. The previous year, Julian's team had been beaten up and robbed. In separate Hindu Kush incidents that year, a British television cameraman had been murdered at his bivouac, an entire tranche of aid money had been stolen from a Swedish mission, and a UN convoy had been hijacked. So, discretion was part of the package.

In a remote valley in the western Himalaya I had sloughed my Western trekking kit and pulled on a baggy *salwar kameez* and flat cap – the Afghan *pukhool*. An unconvincing beard completed the charade. Resting on a pickup bonnet I'd written my will, then pushed it into a brown envelope along with my passport and wallet. Once we had crossed the border into Afghanistan, there would be no contact with the outside world. The pile of dusty clothes on the ground belonged to another person, a privileged tourist who had always seen the wilderness as a natural wonder, who had viewed ethnic diversity as a source of curiosity and comparison. The impending journey would change all that – the mountains ahead of us were a defence system scattered with anti-personnel mines and divided by exposed passes.

For six days we walked and rode on horseback through the mountains, sleeping under the stars or crammed like so many maize cobs into fetid *chaikharnas* (tea houses) whose locations were known to our two guides, Qudous and Jabbar. Both men had grown up in the Panjshir. I'd read of this valley as a teenager, when I'd found in my grandparents' bookshelves a copy of Eric Newby's Afghan adventure *A Short Walk in the Hindu Kush*. Visiting in the 1950s, Newby had depicted the Panjshir as a lost paradise, a place where children played hide and seek in 'enchanted forests' of wheat and corn; a place of heaped apricots and of mulberries which dropped earthward 'in an endless shower'. Newby wrote of poplar groves and dappled willows; of families happily threshing; of women in pretty blues and reds and of little boys in embroidered hats. It was, Newby recalled, 'like some golden age of human happiness, attained sometimes by children, more rarely by grown-ups, and it communicated its magic in some degree to all of us.'

On 7 September we walked the horses down from the final pass into the Panjshir village of Dashte Rewat. Among the bomb craters and roofless houses there was little movement. Every wall was pitted with bullets and shrapnel. Where trees had once shaded the way, there were now rows of stumps. Mutilated beyond belief, Newby's paradise had been pulverised by eight Soviet offensives in 10 years. Of the Panjshir's prewar population of 29,000 families, only about 7000 remained, hidden away in the more remote reaches of the valley.

We slept on the roof of the Mujahideen Hotel and in the morning hitched a ride down the valley in a captured Soviet jeep. Whole villages had been reduced to rubble and dust. Burned-out tanks, armoured personnel carriers and trucks were scattered around the valley floor. A bridge we crossed had been fashioned from a salvaged lorry chassis and sections of tank track.

For the next three weeks we walked and rode up and down the Panjshir, interviewing village headmen and conducting our census of destruction. In village after village we listened to tales of savagery and fortitude. The Soviets had systematically mined the irrigation channels or blasted them from the cliffs. There was a desperate shortage of seed, of timber, of oxen, of water. One man we met had run from his house as the bombs fell. When he looked back, a vast crater occupied the site of his house. Another villager had rebuilt his house four times. And, he said, he would rebuild it next time it was flattened. Miras Abdullah, a mullah from the village of Rockha, had once had 10 in his family. One son had been killed and another had lost a leg when he stood on a mine. Before the war, his livestock had included two cows and an ox, 10 sheep, one donkey and six goats. 'Now I have no animals,' he told us, 'and I am living under canvas.' His story was typical. Our notebooks filled with lists of loss. And occasional humour: 'Before the war,' said Mohammed Rasi, 'I had nine in my family and I had one horse, one donkey, 20 goats, 10 sheep and three cows. Now, my house is completely destroyed and the only animals I have left are one horse and one donkey. My main problem is that I need a Mercedes-Benz.'

We worked hard, pushing the survey close to the Soviet front line and riding far into side valleys. The travelling had a harmonious equivalence: as a traveller, I felt that I was paying my dues, giving as much as I was taking. The surprise lunch of spring onions and chapatis with the headman of a shattered village could be enjoyed with unequivocal rapture; we had earned that meal in sweat and dysentery. But the guilt was always there, the guilt of the privileged voyeur observing misery: I could leave the Hindu Kush for a home in London; the refugees of the Panjshir could choose between battlefield dust or camps in Pakistan.

The survey was completed by the end of September. Work done, it remained for us to extract ourselves from the Hindu Kush with our notebooks before the onset of winter. In leaving the Panjshir, we would become recipients rather than donors of goodwill. Our maps were inadequate to get ourselves out without help, and we had insufficient food and no tents. We would be dependent upon many random kindnesses, and upon our two guides – and friends – Qudous and Jabbar.

The plan had been to return to the outside world by way of a long detour through the northern valleys of the Hindu Kush. We'd begin by crossing the Parendeh Pass to Andarab, where there were rumours of fighting between the mujahedin and government forces. London wanted to know whether Andarab was calm enough to receive aid. From Andarab, we would have to cross five more passes before we could leave the country. The journey out would take 14 days of riding, walking and climbing. There was a chill in the air. Winter had come early. With a brittle excitement, we took to the trail.

Our flight from the Hindu Kush began ominously. Coming down into Andarab's valley we passed the corpse of a villager who had just been shot. And at dusk, as we crouched over the BBC World Service news, a man on the other side of our window fired his Kalashnikov towards neighbouring houses. The cold evening recoiled to sporadic explosions and shots. By morning, one of our horses was missing. Andarab was not 'calm'. We left early.

A couple of days later we crossed the Suchi Pass and arrived for the night at a small hamlet. In a room floored with straw, the eight of us shared a large bowl of rice and then a volcano of mashed bread surrounded by a moat of ghee. By morning, snow was falling.

The horses hated the snow, and the next pass was steep. Cold and tired, we plodded mechanically up the mountainside on a thin, muddy trail through bleak mists. As the trail climbed higher, the wind blew harder, plastering our worn cotton combat jackets with snow and coating beards in tendrils of ice. That night we crammed into a tiny hut and ate cold rice in the dark. The talk was of passes and, in particular, of the Kafir Kotal, the greatest obstacle on our escape route through the Hindu Kush. If it proved to be iced, the horsemen would not be able to cross.

Our little troupe withdrew into individual cocoons. After weeks of concentrating on completing our survey, I was now obsessively concerned with my own skin. Life had been reduced to two selfish issues: would the passes get blocked with snow before we could reach them, and where would the next food come from? There was little to be done about the former anxiety, except to encourage the general notion that we should walk and ride for as many hours of each day as was physically possible. The food issue depended upon the ability of Qudous and Jabbar to procure rations at the sporadic *chaikharnas* and hamlets along the trail. There were occasional, mouthwatering surprises. In a bazaar, Qudous managed to find a huge bowl of soup into which chunks of bread were mashed. The eight of us scooped hungrily at the sludge with our fingers. At another trail halt, eggs appeared. In a village set on a green lawn below a bright wall of icy peaks, one man welcomed us with tea and small, hard doughnuts. I greeted each of these unexpected treats with pathetic outpourings of gratitude.

Every day the snow line crept lower down the mountain flanks. As we rode and walked eastward, we began to gather rumours of trouble on the passes ahead. An Afghan struggled into a *chaikharna* with news that people were turning back from the Wishti Pass. And then Qudous heard on the 'talkie-walkie' (the trail's word-of-mouth message relay) of a great storm that had killed five men and over 100 horses on the Kafir Kotal.

At the foot of the Wishti, we unexpectedly came to a *chaikharna,* a shadowy, warm cave of a place. Cross-legged we sat on a goat-coloured carpet and sipped tea from china bowls. Jabbar handed out dried mulberries to chew on the climb. 'For the mountain,' he smiled, pressing his forehead.

Devilled with stomach cramps, I suffered on the Wishti and got left far behind the horses. We came down the pass to another *chaikharna* and I slumped against the wall of a long, thin room while Qudous boiled rice in the cold. The 'talkie-walkie' had revised its death toll on the Kafir Kotal to 230 horses and mules. The only alternative to the Kafir Kotal was a longer, lower detour through a valley whose trails were still mined.

It took us two more days to reach the foot of the Kafir Kotal. By a frozen stream in a lightless defile, the mujahedin had erected a pair of tents. The tents were packed with horsemen, refugees and fighters. This was the pass which would divide those who would winter in Afghanistan from those who would winter in Pakistan. Two of our horsemen decided not to risk the pass. We dumped clothing and our medical kit to lighten our packs.

For breakfast somebody shared a few slices of old bread and part of a tin of Pakistani cheese. Then we stepped into the snow.

The approach to the pass was far from straightforward. We had to cross a minefield and then, to avoid more mines, negotiate an awkward traverse across the bald face of a cliff. At a crashed Russian helicopter we paused for a rest, and then began the final climb through the snowclouds.

Late in the afternoon, we emerged into a high, desolate valley. Ahead of us rose the snow-covered head wall of the valley and at its top, the notch which marked the crest of the Kafir Kotal. Zigzags of men and animals were struggling up a polished groove of ice and snow that had been worn into the head wall. Beside the zigzags, a single chute fell from top to bottom, and down this chute tumbled crates of ammunition, rocket-propelled grenades and sacks of grain – all manner of burden released from the top of the pass by an incoming convoy confronted by an impossible descent.

Clawing up the snow beside the zigzags, I was nearly bowled down the head wall by a cartwheeling mule. Scrabbling horses were being anchored by men with ropes. When I fell myself, sliding and spinning downward, I grabbed at a passing rock jutting from the snow, only to find that it was the frozen head of a horse.

In the chaos of that pass I lost the others and it was nearly dark when I lurched into the *chaikharna* on the far side of the Kafir Kotal. Qudous was already there, and he handed me a pint of tea and a bowl of rice. Later, Jabbar and Julian staggered into the *chaikharna*. Jabbar's feet were a mess. Qudous insisted that we press on. Now down to four, he led the way, down, down, down. Long after dark, we stumbled into a large, spotlessly carpeted tent. Another temporary *chaikharna,* this one run by Nuristanis. Somehow, they knocked up a meal of boiled rice and tender chunks of meat. By morning our two remaining horsemen were with us.

The next day there was another pass. The last climb, it marked the border between Afghanistan and Pakistan. In blinding sunlight, we walked through deep pillows of new snow. Behind us, the entire horizon was jewelled with diamond peaks.

Qudous led the way down, into a long, cold valley. And it was here, in the floor of that valley, that we found the low stone shelter. The final leg of the journey required a mujahedin guide to lead us through the cliffs to the valley far below. 'You wait here,' said Qudous. 'I will go ahead and arrange for the guide.'

So we waited at the shelter. Qudous had promised to find a guide. And he would.

ASCENSION IN THE MOONLIGHT
SIMON WINCHESTER

Simon Winchester, a former geologist and foreign correspondent for the *Guardian*, now lives in America, dividing his time between Manhattan and a farm in the Berkshire Hills of Massachusetts. He is the author of the best-selling *The Surgeon of Crowthorne* (published in the US as *The Professor and the Madman*), *The Map That Changed the World*, *Krakatoa* and numerous other books. His most recent book is *Bomb, Book and Compass* (published in the US as *The Man Who Loved China*).

IT WAS A BLAZING TROPICAL MORNING in the middle of nowhere. I was on a rusting, salt-stained Russian tramp steamer beating slowly up towards England across the doldrums, and for reasons long forgotten I was in a desperate hurry to get home. We were making no more than eight knots that day, which meant that I'd not see the cranes of any European port for the better part of three more weeks. And out there on those hot high seas – I was on my way back from Antarctica – it was unutterably tedious.

The radar on the bridge showed an Atlantic Ocean surrounding us, entirely empty of everything – except, that is, for the tiny speck of Ascension Island, which lay otherwise invisible, 65 kilometres off, on our starboard bow. It was then, in a sudden moment of realisation, that I remembered something. On Ascension Island there was an airfield, and jet planes flew there, to and from London. If I played my cards right, *I could get myself out of here.*

I promptly got on the ship's radio, asking if anyone over on Ascension could possibly hear me. At first, nothing – just the hissing white silence of dead ocean air. But I called and I called, and eventually, quite faintly at first, there came over the ether a British voice. Yes, it said, he was the duty harbour master. What did I need? I told him I wanted to get on the next RAF flight to Britain, and so could I come and land on Ascension and try and wangle my way aboard?

Yes, he replied, after a momentary muffled conversation with someone else, provided that I was fit and able to jump when told to do so – because the Atlantic rollers were making landing at Ascension perilous that day – it should be possible for me to land; and since there was a northbound plane due to arrive in two days, then I might also be able to find a seat and get myself to London in double-quick time. 'Ask your captain to steer towards Ascension,' the man said, 'and when 800 metres off, tell him to put you ashore in the whaler. If you're fit,' he said with what sounded like a sinister chuckle, 'you ought to be able to make it.'

Half a day's slow sailing later, and the enormous dark pyramid of Ascension Island rose up directly ahead of us – a mid-ocean volcano, 800 metres high, its summit brushed with green foliage and a patch of dark cloud, the slopes and the spreading base iron-grey coloured and seemingly as lifeless as the moon. A few sorry-looking buildings were dotted here and there, and a cluster of radar domes and aerials, and there was a gathering of Nissan huts around the long single runway of the aerodrome.

A grinning Russian sailor who said he had been here once before, and who the captain assured me 'knew the form', lowered me into his whaler, and we motored swiftly off across the chop. We chugged away from the rusty little ship, across to a tiny gap in the Ascension sea wall, a gap in which I could see a narrow set of steps rising up slimily from the waves. Enormous swells and rollers crashed over these steps at regular intervals, completely immersing them, then draining away again in a rush of wild whitewater and fronds of streaming weed. There was a slime-covered rope fasted to a doubtful-looking and very corroded iron stanchion. The Russian told me that all I had to do was to wait for the interval between swells, leap onto the highest step I could manage – the higher I managed, the less slippery the steps, he laughed – and clutch hold of the rope as tightly as I could.

Well, I'm here today, and so the scheme must have worked. All I remember is a welter of confused green water, the precipitous dipping and rising of our whaler's bow, the sudden scream from behind me of 'Now!', my feet and hands scrambling for a hold, the wet length of rope tightening under my weight, the onrushing of the next wave knocking me off balance but the rope holding, holding – and then my furious dash upwards until I was at last onto a dry step. My bag, hurled with great force by the Russian sailor way down below, landed roughly beside me, followed by the yell of *Dosvidanya!* from behind.

And then, quietly, almost like a gentle whisper from my left, came another voice.

'Do let me be the first to welcome you to the British colony of

Ascension Island,' it said. 'My name is Paul Wilson. I am the vicar here. And this is my wife, Angela.'

I turned, and indeed there was, quite unexpectedly, a cleric – a young, fresh-faced clergyman very obviously of the Church of England, dressed in white shorts and a tropical shirt, but with the telltale clerical collar. He was short, fair-haired, very pinkish, precise, rimlessly bespectacled.

The Reverend Paul Wilson, vicar of Saint Mary's, wore an expression that morning of a sincerely concerned kindliness – as did his wife, who looked rather like him, only she was larger and somewhat gawky in a sundress of an old-fashioned chintz print, such that unkind souls might say she looked a little like a small, animated sofa. The pair could not have been anything other than English, two expatriates doing their level best to find suitable employment for themselves during the languid hours of faraway tropical heat. Meeting me, I guessed, was part of what they might have called their *pastoral duties,* ensuring that all was well with their flock on this tiny outpost of what remained of Britain's empire, here in the outermost reaches of an otherwise unpopulated stretch of ocean.

I shook hands, and Paul suggested that I step along towards their house. It was a 500-metre walk to Saint Mary's vicarage, a walk which took us past the old fever hospital and the former lazaretto for African lepers, and past the 19th-century barracks that had housed Royal Marines who were stationed on Ascension to make doubly sure that Napoleon would stay put, in his permanent post-Waterloo exile on Saint Helena, a few hundred kilometres to our south.

It was far too hot today, and there was no one about – just a few donkeys, now wild animals that plagued the island just like the feral cats the local people had tried to eliminate some years before. The donkeys chewed the wing mirrors off the local cars, and everybody loathed them.

We walked past the tiny modern bungalow where the administrator worked – no colonial governor was warranted on so small a dependency as this, said Reverend Paul. Then in a low voice he explained that most administrators were men who had 'rather failed to make an impression' during their careers in Britain's diplomatic service.

It was the only unkind thing I ever heard Paul say, though it was evident that neither he nor Angela seemed much to like their posting on the island. Paul had been preaching quite happily, thank you, in a church in Spitalfields in London, when orders had appeared one Monday in the post, suggesting that he might like to take over the Church of Saint Mary's of the High Seas in the Dependency of Ascension. It was a three-year job; there were 200 people on the island, most of them Saint Helenians working on contract for the airbase, or else secretive expatriates working among the fields of aerials, performing hush-hush work for one of the American spy agencies.

'They call the Saint Helenians "Saints",' said Paul as he opened his garden gate. 'So I imagine they don't really need us, do they?' He chuckled mildly at his own drollery. 'And the Americans don't come to our church. So Angela and I have rather little to do – and frankly we see almost no one. Which is why we were so pleased when they said you were stopping by. You are more than welcome to have lunch, and then please stay with us until the plane comes in tomorrow night.'

Inside there was a salad waiting for me, and a glass of cold beer. 'I expect you'll be very happy with that,' he said, and he winked at his wife conspiratorially, as if a drink at lunchtime was somehow mildly sinful.

And so I stayed in their little rectory for the rest of that day and night, chatting and indulging in what passes for Ascension tourism – which means, primarily, climbing to the top of Green Mountain, then going for a swim in the dewpond at the summit, and signing my name in what must be one of the least-used visitors' books on the planet. From high up on top of the mountain, if the clouds part for long enough, it is possible to see 100 kilometres in all directions, and the ocean – looking like an unblemished sheet of hammered pewter – stretched empty to every horizon. It was so lonely that I almost shuddered.

During the night the southbound air force jet had come in, on its way down to the Falkland Islands, and so the following morning we had English newspapers and magazines, and I was able to catch up with news and gossip. I had been in the Southern Ocean for the better part of the previous four months, and knew little of the goings-on up north; and now, reading all about it, so much seemed so blessedly irrelevant. Angela was happy, though, and spent her day in the garden contentedly buried in the *Daily Mail* and a copy of the *Tatler*, lobbing pebbles at any donkeys that tried to eat her sandwiches.

Once she looked up from her reverie, and spoke to me. She had a surprise for me later that night, she said with a smile – she would give it to me just before I left. The northbound plane – Paul had managed to get me a seat on it, as had been suggested on the ship's radio – was due in a little before two in the morning. Perhaps, Angela said, if we all took a little siesta – something not too difficult to achieve, in a place that was hot, lonely and exceptionally boring – we could all arrange to go down to the airfield together, and they would see me off. I protested that there was really no need, but they seemed to want to. They apparently had something planned.

I must have slept until 10. It was quite dark when I awoke, and the house was alive with a curiously expectant air. Downstairs I found Paul and Angela dressed in mufti – no dog-collar or chintz, but swimming costumes instead – and packing up a picnic basket. 'Well done, waking now,' said Paul cheerfully. 'We thought we'd go off on an expedition. We'll take you to the only white-sand beach on the island – and when we're there I think we'll see something rather special.

'And by the way – I think Angela said something about a surprise? Well, they came on the jet from England. Fresh strawberries and Devonshire cream! We've not had them for a year! And you've probably gone without such things for ages. So let's take them down to the sea, right away!'

And so, after I had changed into my trunks, we set off in their rickety old Morris Minor – the car that they and their predecessors had all inherited from a vicar back in the '60s – and we swept slowly around the island, past the old colonial buildings and the great airfield and the Nissan huts, until we turned off and bumped down through a rocky defile, and along to a tiny beach, glinting pure white under a fast-rising moon.

As it rose, the soft and sugary sand took on an appearance just like snow – the sea beyond it black, its waves crashing rhythmically on the shore, the rocks behind black also, and in between them this postcard-sized field of the purest white shell powder, illuminated by the immense pale moon, and with a clear sky full of a blizzard of stars.

Angela unpacked the hamper, and she laid out dishes of strawberries and a jug of cream on the blanket, together with three glasses and a bottle of cool white wine. To sharpen our appetite, and to delay the pleasure of the food, we all ran down to the sea and swam for a while, then lay floating beyond the surf, the water warm and velvet soft, and we gazed up at the sky, looking for shooting stars. After 15 minutes or so Paul looked at his watch. 'Back to the beach!' he cried. 'The show starts soon.'

I had no idea what he meant, but the three of us walked back up to where we had left our things, and sat back and toasted one another with Vouvray and ate the soft fruit and the cool cream, and joked with one another that we were, as Paul and Angela must have known, in some anteroom to heaven. And then Paul cried out.

'Look!' he said, and pointed down to where the waves were crashing onto the beach. 'Quiet!'

I saw it in an instant. It quite startled me. A huge dark shape was lumbering slowly out of the white water, and was heading, inching, up the beach. First one emerged, then another, and another – until there were maybe 15 of them, moving slowly and almost painfully up the sloping sand, like wounded soldiers of an invasion force. One of them approached within two metres of us – and once so close, I could see exactly what it was.

A green turtle. I had heard about them – Brazilian green turtles, living on Brazil's Atlantic coast and yet choosing, due to some curious quirk of nature, to lay their eggs 3000 kilometres away on this tiny island in the middle of their ocean. And this, precisely, was what each one of these huge, magnificent beasts was doing.

The lady closest to us turned ponderously around so that she was facing the sea, then used her back flippers to scoop out a cavity in the sand. Once it was 90 centimetres or so deep, she quietened herself and concentrated, until, with a strangely, unforgettably intimate sound of chelonian parturition, she expelled a clutch of 30 or 40 eggs into the hole. I craned myself up quietly and saw the eggs as they lay, glistening wetly in the moonlight, until their patient mother shovelled sand back on top of them, to protect them and keep them dry.

She seemed utterly exhausted from the effort, quite drained, and for a few understandable moments she rested, until, with what in a man would have been a quite superhuman effort of will, she hoisted herself back down the slope, battered her weary way through the raging surf, and began her long, slow, eggless swim back home again, all the way to Brazil.

For fully an hour the three of us watched, transfixed. Occasionally I could see that Paul was watching me, just to make certain that I was as enraptured as he had been when first he saw the animals. Angela spoke softly as she poured another glass of wine. 'Aren't we just the luckiest people?' she said. 'Isn't this a privilege?'

But that wasn't the half of it. There was more. For at almost the same moment as she asked this rhetorical question, she shivered. I could see her skin was suddenly covered with goose bumps. She drew a beach towel around her shoulders. And I felt it too – a sudden coldness in the air, as though a cloud had materialised from the tropical sky, and blanketed everything in its chill.

But it wasn't a cloud. As I looked up at the moon I could see that the shadow of the earth was now steadily sweeping across its face, and the whole world was darkening again, being turned back to black as this portion of our planet experienced a total lunar eclipse. Suddenly the white sand went dark. I could no longer see Paul or Angela. Only the glow of the distant runway lights spoke of civilisation nearby. Only those lights, and the stars, broke the velvet blackness of the night.

As I looked at the stars I suddenly noticed something else: that in the eastern sky, rising above the dark where the horizon had been, was a bright object that, once I could see it properly, was undeniably *a comet*. A famous, swept-tailed comet, blazing for thousands of miles out in some distant part of the solar system, and now only properly visible because the air was so clear here, and the local world was so inkily black. It was splendid, unbelievably so.

The moon came out of its shadow a few moments later, and the brilliance of the stars faded a little, and the comet became barely visible once again. But just then it had been visible, and I, moreover, had seen it.

And it was in that instant I realised something: that in this astonishing grand conjunction – of new friendship, of tropical warmth, of strawberries and cream and cool white wine, of white sand and sea swimming, and of Brazilian turtles, an eclipse of the moon and the rising of a comet – was perhaps the greatest wealth of experience that any one individual could ever know in one moment. I was at that instant blessed beyond belief, beyond all understanding. And that state of grace had all come about purely and simply because one man and one woman – the Reverend Paul Wilson and his comfortable wife Angela, who had been perfect strangers to me until now – had decided to offer me, for one unrewarded moment, no more and no less than their kindness.

And yet of course their kindness *was* rewarded, and more handsomely than is conceivable. For neither they, nor I, will ever be able to forget it. Virtue is its own reward, I thought to myself, a reward written here for eternity on this tiny unremembered island.

Then the mood altered, as it always must, for after a few minutes two brilliant searchlights appeared low on the horizon, and they grew steadily brighter every passing second. For a moment I thought it was the comet again; but Paul jumped up. He had seen it before. 'Your plane,' he announced. 'We'd better hurry.'

My jet landed the next morning at an airbase in the Cotswolds, and I decided on a whim, having an hour or two now to spare, that on my way down to London I would stop in and see my Oxford tailor. So at about 10 o'clock I was standing in the fitting room, and before he slipped the new jacket on me, he asked me to unroll my shirtsleeves. As I did so, a cascade of the purest white sand fell from the folds, onto the carpet. I apologised, but the tailor said it was no trouble, and asked, more out of politeness than serious inquiry, whether I could tell him where it had come from. Ascension Island, I said, and proceeded to tell him the story.

He listened patiently, and then, putting away his chalk and looping his tape around his neck, he said, 'You know, you are a very, very lucky man indeed. Lucky to be in such a place. Lucky to see such things. And luckiest of all to meet such very kind people. I envy you. Everyone must envy you. Wherever would you be – have you ever wondered? – without all their kindness, and without all this luck?' As he opened the door for me he put his hand briefly on my shoulder. And then I walked off into the rain.